William M. Lawrence, O Blackman

The Riverside Song Book

Containing classic American Poems set to standard Music

William M. Lawrence, O Blackman

The Riverside Song Book
Containing classic American Poems set to standard Music

ISBN/EAN: 9783337240837

Printed in Europe, USA, Canada, Australia, Japan

Cover: Foto ©Thomas Meinert / pixelio.de

More available books at **www.hansebooks.com**

The Riverside Literature Series

THE RIVERSIDE SONG BOOK

CONTAINING CLASSIC AMERICAN POEMS
SET TO STANDARD MUSIC

SELECTED AND ARRANGED BY

W. M. LAWRENCE

PRINCIPAL OF THE RAY SCHOOL, CHICAGO

AND

O. BLACKMAN

SUPERVISOR OF VOCAL MUSIC IN THE PUBLIC SCHOOLS OF CHICAGO

HOUGHTON, MIFFLIN AND COMPANY
Boston: 4 Park Street; New York: 11 East Seventeenth Street
Chicago: 378-388 Wabash Avenue
The Riverside Press, Cambridge

The Riverside Press, Cambridge, Mass., U. S. A.
Electrotyped and Printed by H. O. Houghton & Company.

PREFACE.

THIS collection has been prepared mainly for use in schools. Believing that in the preparation of school song books too little attention has been paid to the character of the words sung, we have made our selections for the most part from the writings of American poets of high standing. With these before us, we have sought for music of an equally high order with which to wed the words, and where we have introduced old and familiar songs, we have edited the music with care. In nearly all the part songs, the melody can be sung alone with good effect. We desire to acknowledge our special indebtedness to Professor C. E. R. Mueller for valuable aid rendered in the work of musical revision.

The several indexes with which the book is provided record the contents, and show the origin of the words and the music. By means of the Topical Index, the teacher may readily discover the adaptability of the book to those special occasions, like national holidays and birthday celebrations, which form an important element in school life.

We submit the result of our work to teachers and superintendents, with the hope that it may strengthen in our schools that spirit of loyalty to American ideals already nobly expressed in American poetry.

W. M. LAWRENCE.
O. BLACKMAN.

TABLE OF CONTENTS.

INDEX OF AUTHORS.

TOPICAL INDEX.

The following classification is intended to be merely suggestive. In celebrating the birthday of an author not represented in this collection, select songs that are in harmony with the writer's work. Thus, for example, songs relating to the sea, to Indian life, and to the American Revolution, may be used for James Fenimore Cooper; songs of nature would be appropriate for Henry David Thoreau, especially those by Emerson, his intimate friend.

Acknowledgment is due to the following publishers and authors for permission to use the poems contained in this volume controlled or written by them : —

Messrs. D. Appleton & Co.	W. C. Bryant.
Messrs. Charles Scribner's Sons	Sidney Lanier, R. H. Stoddard.
The Century Co.	R. W. Gilder.
J. B. Lippincott Co.	T. Buchanan Read.
Cassell Publishing Co.	J. Boyle O'Reilly.
Horace L. Traubel	Walt Whitman.
Eugene Field.	
Joaquin Miller.	

The music of the following songs is used by arrangement with The Oliver Ditson Co.: Keller's American Hymn (Angel of Peace), Foster's Old Folks at Home (Swanee River), Kittredge's Tenting on the Old Camp Ground, Webster's Don't be sorrowful, Darling, Emerson's Reaper and the Flowers, Pike's Home Again, Mason's Nearer, My God, to Thee, Woodbury's Stars of the Summer Night, Foster's My Own shall come to Me, and Paine's Centennial Hymn. Root's "There's Music in the Air" is used by arrangement with The John Church Co.

THE
RIVERSIDE SONG BOOK.

MY COUNTRY, 'T IS OF THEE.

Samuel Francis Smith.
Moderato.

Unknown.
(Air: God Save the King.)

1. My coun-try, 'tis of thee, Sweet land of lib - er - ty,
2. My na - tive coun - try, thee—Land of the no - ble free—
3. Let mu - sic swell the breeze, And ring from all the trees
4. Our fa - thers' God, to Thee, Au - thor of lib - er - ty,

Of thee I sing; Land where my fa - thers died, Land of the
Thy name I love; I love thy rocks and rills, Thy woods and
Sweet free-dom's song; Let mor - tal tongues a-wake; Let all that
To Thee we sing; Long may our land be bright With free - dom's

Pil-grim's pride; From ev - 'ry mountain side, Let free - dom ring.
tem - pled hills; My heart with rap - ture thrills, Like that a - bove.
breathe partake; Let rocks their si - lence break—The sound pro - long.
ho - ly light: Pro - tect us by Thy might, Great God, our King.

(1)

Oliver Wendell Holmes.

Carl Wilhelm.
(Air: Die Wacht am Rhein.)

Maestoso.

1. What flow'r is this that greets the morn, Its hues from heav'n so
2. In sav - age Na - ture's far a - bode Its ten - der seed our
3. Be - hold its streaming rays u - nite, One mingling flood of
4. The blades of he - roes fence it round, Where'er it springs is
5. Thy sa - cred leaves, fair Free-dom's flow'r, Shall ev - er float on

fresh - ly born? With burn - ing star and flam - ing band It
fa - thers sowed; The storm-winds rocked its swell - ing bud,- Its
braid - ed light,— The red that fires the South - ern rose, With
ho - ly ground; From tower and dome its glo - ries spread; It
dome and tower, To all their heav'n-ly col - ors true, In

kin - dles all the sun - set land: O tell us what its
op'n - ing leaves were streaked with blood, Till lo! earth's ty - rants
spot - less white from north - ern snows, And, span - gled o'er its
waves where lone - ly sen - tries tread; It makes the land as
black'n-ing frost or crim - son dew,— And God love us as

mf

name may be,— Is this the Flower of Lib - er - ty?
shook to see The full - blown Flower of Lib - er - ty!
az - ure, see The sis - ter Stars of Lib - er - ty!
o - cean free, And plants an em - pire on the sea!
we love thee, Thrice ho - ly Flower of Lib - er - ty!

It Is, It Is the ban - ner of the free,
Then hail, then hail the ban - ner of the free,
Then hail, then hail the ban - ner of the free,
Then hail, then hail the ban - ner of the free,
Then hail, then hail the ban - ner of the free,

The star - ry Flower, the Flower of Lib - er - ty!
The star - ry Flower, the Flower of Lib - er - ty!
The star - ry Flower, the Flower of Lib - er - ty!
The star - ry Flower, the Flower of Lib - er - ty!
The star - ry Flower, the Flower of Lib - er - ty!

TRUE FREEDOM.

James Russell Lowell.

Friedrich Silcher.

1. Men! whose boast it is that ye Come of fa - thers brave and free,
2. Is true free - dom but to break Fet - ters for our own dear sake,
3. They are slaves who fear to speak For the fall - en and the weak;

If there breathe on earth a slave, Are ye tru - ly free and brave?
And, with leath - ern hearts, for-get That we owe man - kind a debt?
They are slaves who will not choose Ha - tred, scoff-ing, and a - buse,

If ye do not feel the chain, When it works an - oth - er's pain,
No! true freedom is to share All the chains our broth-ers wear,
Rath - er than in si - lence shrink From the truth they needs must think;

Are ye not base slaves in - deed, Slaves un-wor - thy to be freed?
And, with heart and hand, to be Ear - nest to make oth - ers free!
They are slaves who dare not be In the right with two or three.

William Cullen Bryant.

German Air.
(Air: Der Tannenbaum.)

Maestoso.

1. Lay down the axe; fling by the spade; Leave in its track the toiling plough;
2. Come ye, who breast the mountain storm By grassy steep or highland lake,
3. Come ye, who throng be - side the deep, Her ports and hamlets of the strand,

The ri - fle and the bayo - net blade For arms like yours were fit-ter now;
Come, for the land ye love, to form A bul - wark that no foe can break.
In num-ber like the waves that leap On his long-murm 'ring marge of sand;

Ho! stur-dy as the oaks ye cleave, And moved as soon to fear and flight;
And ye whose homes are by the grand Swift riv - ers, ris - ing far a - way,
Few, few were they whose swords of old Won the fair land in which we dwell;
D.S. *Strike for our broad and good - ly land, Blow aft - er blow, till men shall see*

Fine. D.S.

Men of the glade and for - est! leave Your woodcraft for the field of fight.
Come from the depth of your green land, As mighty in your march as they.
But we are ma - ny, we who hold The grim re-solve to guard it well.
That might and right move hand in hand, And glo-rious must their tri - umph be.

D.S.

SAIL ON, O SHIP OF STATE!

Henry Wadsworth Longfellow.   German Air.

1. Sail on, sail on, O Ship of State! Sail on, sail
2. We know what Mas - ter laid thy keel, Sail on, sail
3. Fear not each sud - den sound and shock, Sail on, sail
4. Sail on, sail on, O Ship of State! Sail on, sail

on!   Sail   on,   O   Un - ion   strong   and
on!   What Work - man wrought thy   ribs   of
on!   'T is of   the   wave   and   not   the
on!   Sail   on,   O   Un - ion   strong   and

great, Sail on, sail on!   Hu - man - i - ty   with
steel, Sail on, sail on!   Who made each mast, and
rock; Sail on, sail on!   'T is but the flap - ping
great, Sail on, sail on!   Sail on, nor fear to

all   its fears, With all the hopes of fu - ture years, Is
sail, and rope, What an - vils rang, what ham - mers beat. In
of   the sail, And not a rent made by the gale! In
breast the sea, Our hearts, our hopes, are all with thee, Our

hanging breathless on thy fate! Sail on, O UN-ION, strong and great! Sail
what a forge and what a heat Were shaped the anchors of thy hope! Sail
spite of rock and tempest's roar, In spite of false lights on the shore, Sail
hearts, our hopes, our prayers, our tears, Our faith triumphant o'er our fears, Are

on, sail on, O Ship of State, Sail on, sail on!
on, sail on, O Ship of State, Sail on, sail on!
on, sail on, O Ship of State, Sail on, sail on!
all with thee,—Are all with thee! Sail on, sail on!

THE POOR VOTER ON ELECTION DAY.

John Greenleaf Whittier.   German Air.

Maestoso.

1. The proud-est now is but my peer, The high-est not more
2. Who serves to - day up - on the list Be - side the served shall
3. To - day let pomp and vain pre - tense My stub - born right a -
4. While there's a grief to seek re - dress, Or bal - ance to ad -

high; . . The high - est not more high; To-
stand; . Be - side the served shall stand; A -
bide; . . . . My stub - born right a - bide; I
just, ... Or bal - ance to ad - just, Where

day, of all the wea-ry year, A king of men am I.
like the brown and wrinkled fist, The gloved and dain - ty hand!
set a plain man's common sense A - gainst the ped - ant's pride.
weighs our liv - ing manhood less Than Mammon's vil - est dust,—

To - day, a - like are great and small, The name-less and the known; My
The rich is lev - el with the poor, The weak is strong to-day; The
To - day shall simple man-hood try The strength of gold and land; The
While there's a right to need my vote, A wrong to sweep a - way, Up!

pal - ace is the peo - ple's hall, The bal - lot - box my throne!
sleek-est broadcloth counts no more Than home - spun frock of gray.
wide world has not wealth to buy The power in my right hand!
clout-ed knee and rag - ged coat! A man's a man to - day!

Ralph Waldo Emerson. **Ludwig van Beethoven.**

1. By the rude bridge that arched the flood, Their flag to A - pril's
2. On this green bank, by this soft stream, We set to - day a

breeze un - furled, Here once th' em-bat - tled farm-ers stood, And
vo - tive stone; That mem-'ry may their deed re - deem, When,

fired the shot heard round the world. The foe long since in
like our sires, our sons are gone. Spir - it, that made those

si - lence slept; A - like the con - queror si - lent sleeps; And
he - roes dare To die, and leave their chil - dren free, Bid

Time the ru - in'd bridge has swept Down the dark stream which sea-ward creeps.
Time and Na-ture gen - tly spare The shaft we raise to them and thee.

THE FALCON.

James Russell Lowell.   Friedrich Silcher.

mp

1. I know a fal - con swift and peer - less As
2. No harm - less dove, no bird that sing - eth,
3. Let fraud and wrong and base - ness shiv - er, For

mf   *cres.*

e'er was cra - dled in the pine; No bird had ev - er
Shud - ders to see him o - ver head; The rush of his fierce
still be - tween them and the sky The fal - con Truth hangs

eye so fear - less, Or wing so strong as this of
swoop - ing bring - eth To in - no - cent hearts no thrill of
poised for - ev - er And marks them with his venge - ful

dim.

mine. Or wing so strong as this of mine.
dread. To in - no - cent hearts no thrill of dread.
eye, And marks them with his venge - ful eye.

Oliver Wendell Holmes.

Unknown.
(Air: Andreas Hofer.)

Maestoso.

cres.

1. Ay, tear the tat-tered en-sign down! Long has it waved on high,
2. Her deck, once red with he-roes' blood, Where knelt the vanquished foe,
3. O bet-ter that her shat-tered hulk Should sink beneath the wave;

And many an eye has danced to see That ban-ner in the sky;
When winds were hurrying o'er the flood, And waves were white be-low,
Her thun-ders shook the might-y deep, And there should be her grave.

Be-neath it rung the bat-tle shout, And burst the can-non's roar;—
No more shall feel the vic-tor's tread, Or know the conquered knee;—
Nail to the mast her ho-ly flag, Set ev - 'ry thread-bare sail,

The me-teor of the o-cean air Shall sweep the clouds no more!
The har-pies of the shore shall pluck The ea - gle of the sea!
And give her to the god of storms, The light-ning and the gale!

The me-teor of the o-cean air Shall sweep the clouds no more!
The har-pies of the shore shall pluck The ea - gle of the sea!
And give her to the god of storms, The light-ning and the gale!

Joseph Hopkinson.

Alla marcia.

Phyla.

1.   Hail, Co - lum - bia, hap - py land!   Hail, ye he - roes
2.   Im-mor - tal   pa - triots! rise once more; De - fend your rights, de
3.   Sound,   sound the trump of fame,   Let   Wash-ing -
4.   Be-hold the chief who now com - mands, Once more to serve his

heav'n-born band! Who fought and bled in free - dom's cause, Who
fend your shore; Let no rude foe with im - pious hand, Let
ton's great name Ring thro' the world with loud ap - plause, Ring
coun - try stands—The rock on which the storm will beat, The

fought and bled in free-dom's cause, And when the storm of
no rude foe with im pious hand, In - vade the shrine where
thro' the world with loud ap - plause, Let ev - 'ry clime to
rock on which the storm will beat; But arm'd in vir - tue

war was gone En - joy'd the peace your val - or won! Let
sa - cred lies, Of toil and blood the well - earned prize! While
free - dom dear List - en with a joy - ful ear! With
firm and true His hopes are fix'd on heav'n and you! When

in - de - peu- dence be our boast, Ev - er mindful what it cost;
off-'ring peace sin- cere and just, In heav'n we place a man - ly trust, That
e - qual skill, And god-like pow'r He gov - ern'd in the fear - ful hour Of
hope was sink-ing in dis - may, And glooms obscur'd Columbia's day, His

Ev - er grate- ful for the prize, Let its al - tar reach the skies !
truth and jus - tice will pre - vail, And ev - 'ry scheme of bond-age fail.
hor - rid war ; or guides with ease The hap-pier times of hon - est peace.
stead- y mind, from changes free, Re - solv'd on death or lib - er - ty.

Firm, u - ni - ted, let us be, Rally-ing round our lib - er - ty ;
Firm, u - ni - ted, let us be, Rally-ing round our lib - er - ty ;
Firm, u - ni - ted, let us be, Rally-ing round our lib - er - ty ;
Firm, u - ni - ted, let us be, Rally-ing round our lib - er - ty ;

As a band of broth-ers join'd, Peace and safe-ty we shall find.
As a band of broth-ers join'd, Peace and safe-ty we shall find.
As a band of broth-ers join'd, Peace and safe-ty we shall find.
As a band of broth-ers join'd, Peace and safe-ty we shall find.

THE STAR-SPANGLED BANNER.

Francis Scott Key.

Samuel Arnold.

Maestoso.

1. O!   say   can   you   see,   by the dawn's ear - ly   light,
2. On the shore dim - ly   seen thro' the mists of   the   deep,
3. And where is that band who so vaunt - ing - ly swore
4. O!   thus be it e'er when   free - men shall stand

What so proud - ly   we hail'd at   the twi - light's last gleaming.
Where the foe's haugh-ty host in dread si - lence re - pos - es,
That the hav - oc of   war and the bat - tle's con - fu - sion
Be - tween their lov'd homes and the   war's des - o - la - tion;

Whose broad stripes and bright stars thro' the   per - il - ous fight,
What is   that which the   breeze, o'er the   tow - er - ing steep,
A   home and a   coun - try should leave us   no   more?
Blest with vic - t'ry and   peace, may the Heav'n-res - cued land

O'er the   ram - parts we watch'd were so gal - lant - ly streaming?
As   it   fit - ful - ly blows, half con - ceals, half dis - clos - es?
Their   blood has wash'd out their foul foot - steps'pol - lu - tion!
Praise the Pow'r that hath made and pre - serv'd us a   na - tion!

And the rock - ets' red glare, the bombs burst-ing in air,
Now it catch-es the gleam of the morn-ing's first beam,
No ref - uge could save the hire - ling and slave
Then con - quer we must, when our cause it is just,

Gave proof thro' the night that our flag was still there;
In full glo - ry re - flect - ed now shines on the stream;
From the ter - ror of flight or the gloom of the grave,
And this be our mot - to, "In God is our trust;"

O! say does the Star - span - gled Ban - ner yet wave
'Tis the Star-span - gled Ban - ner— O! long may it wave
And the Star - span - gled Ban - ner in tri - umph doth wave
And the Star - span - gled Ban - ner in tri - umph shall wave

O'er the land of the free and the home of the brave?
O'er the land of the free and the home of the brave!
O'er the land of the free and the home of the brave.
O'er the land of the free and the home of the brave.

THE RED, WHITE, AND BLUE.

David T. Shaw.   David T. Shaw.

1. O, Co-lum-bia, the gem of the o-cean, The home of the brave
2. When war winged its wide des-o-la-tion, And threatened the land
3. Old Glo-ry to greet, now come hither, With eyes full of love

and the free, The shrine of each pa-triot's de-vo-tion, A
to de-form, The ark then of free-dom's foun-da-tion, Co-
to the brim, May the wreaths of our he-roes ne'er wither, Nor a

world of-fers hom-age to Thee. Thy mandates make heroes as-
lum-bia rode safe through the storm; With their gar-lands of vic-t'ry a-
star of our Ban-ner grow dim; May the ser-vice u-nit-ed ne'er

sem - ble, When Lib - er - ty's form stands in view; Thy
round her, When so proudly she bore her brave crew; With her
sev - er, But they to our col - ors prove true; The

ban-ners make tyr - an -ny trem-ble, Three cheers for the Red, White, and Blue.
flag proud-ly float-ing be-fore her, Three cheers for the Red, White, and Blue.
Ar-my and Na - vy forev - er, Three cheers for the Red, White, and Blue.

CHORUS.

Three cheers for the Red, White, and Blue, Three
Three cheers for the Red, White, and Blue, Three
Three cheers for the Red, White, and Blue, Three

cheers for the Red, White, and Blue, Thy ban - ners make tyr - an - ny
cheers for the Red, White, and Blue, With her flag proud-ly float - ing be-
cheers for the Red, White, and Blue, The Ar - my and Na - vy for-

trem - ble, Three cheers for the Red, White, and Blue.
fore her, Three cheers for the Red, White, and Blue.
ev - er, Three cheers for the Red, White, and Blue.

Oliver Wendell Holmes.

Unknown.
(Air: Yankee Doodle.)

1. An   eve - ning par - ty,—   on - ly that,   No   for - mal in - vi -
2. How   fast the   strag - glers   join   the throng,   From   stall and   work-shop
3. On,   on   to   where the   tea - ships ride!   And   now their   ranks are
4. O   wo - man, at   the   eve - ning board   So   gra - cious, sweet, and
5. Ah,   lit - tle   dreams the   qui - et dame   Who   piles with rock and
6. Old   char - ters   shriv - el   in   its track,   His   Worship's bench has

ta -   tion,   No   gold - laced coat,   no   stiff   cra - vat,   No
gath -   ered!   The   live - ly   bar - ber   skips a - long   And
form -   ing,—   A   rush, and   up   the   Dartmouth's side   The
purr -   ing,   So   hap - py   while the   tea   is   poured, So
spin -   dle   The   pa - tient flax,   how   great a   flame   Yon
crum -   bled,   It   climbs and   clasps the   un - ion - jack,   Its

feast   in   con - tem - pla -   tion,   No   silk - robed dames, no
leaves a   chin   half   lath -   ered;   The   smith   has flung his
Mo -   hawk band is   swarm -   ing!   See   the   fierce na - tives'
blest   while spoons are   stirr -   ing,   What mar - tyr   can   com
lit -   tle   spark shall   kin -   dle!   The   lur - id   morn - ing
bla -   zoned pomp is   hum -   bled,   The   flags   go   down on

fid - dling band, No flow'rs, no songs, no danc - ing,— A
ham - mer down,—The horse - shoe still is glow - ing; The
what a glimpse Of paint and fur and feath - er, As
pare with thee, The moth - er, wife, or daugh - ter, That
shall re - veal A fire no king can smoth - er Where
land and sea Like corn be - fore the reap - ers; So

tribe of Red men, axe in hand,—Be - hold the guests ad - van - cing!
tru - ant tap - ster at the Crown Has left a beer - cask flow - ing!
all at once the full-grown imps Light on the deck to - geth - er!
night, in - tead of best Bo-hea, Condemned to milk and wa - ter!
Brit - ish flint and Bos - ton steel Have clashed a - gainst each oth - er!
burned the fire that brewed the tea That Bos - ton served her keep - ers!

CHORUS TO EACH VERSE.

No! ne'er was mingled such a draft In pal - ace, hall, or ar - bor, As free - men brewed and ty - rants quaffed That night in Bos - ton Har - bor!

A SONG OF THE FLAG.

M. Woolsey Stryker.

(Air: Yankee Doodle — *each stanza sung to first half of solo.*)

1. Roll a river wide and strong,
   Like the tides a-swinging;
   Lift the joyful floods of song,
   Set the mountains ringing.

CHORUS.

Run the lovely banner high!
   Morning's crimson glory,
Field as blue as God's own sky,
   And every star a story.

2. Drown the guns, outsound the bells,
   In the rocking steeple,
While the chorus throbs and swells
   Of a happy people.
      Cho.   Run the lovely banner, etc.

3. For our darling flag we sing,
   Pride of all the nation,

Flag that never knew a king,
   Freedom's constellation.
      Cho.   Run the lovely banner, etc.

4. Blest be God, fraternal wars
   Once for all are ended,
And the gashes and the scars
   Peace and time have mended.
      Cho.   Run the lovely banner, etc.

5. Massachusetts, Maryland,
   Tennessee, Nebraska,
One, Columbia's daughters stand
   From Georgia to Alaska.
      Cho.   Run the lovely banner, etc.

6. Staff and masthead swing it forth —
   Liberty unblighted,
West and East and South and North
   Evermore united!
      Cho.   Run the lovely banner, etc.

Oliver Wendell Holmes.
Ludwig van Beethoven.
(From the Ninth or Choral Symphony.)

1. Wel-come to the day re - turn-ing, Dear-er still as a - ges flow,
2. Hear the tale of youthful glo - ry, While of Brit-ain's res-cued band,
3. Look! the shad-ow on the di - al, Marks the hour of deadlier strife;
4. Vain is Em -pire's mad temp-ta - tion! Not for him an earthly crown!
5. " By the name that you in - her - it, By the suf- f'rings you re-call,
6. Fa - ther! we whose ears have tin- gled With the dis- cord notes of shame,—

While the torch of faith is burn-ing, Long as free-dom's al- tars glow!
Friend and foe re - peat the sto - ry, Spread his fame o'er sea and land,
Days of ter - ror, years of tri - al, Scourge a na - tion in - to life.
He whose sword has freed a na - tion! Strikes the of - fered sceptre down.
Cher -ish the fra - ter - nal spir - it; Love your coun-try first of all!
We, whose sires their blood have mingled In the bat - tle's thunder flame,—

See the he - ro whom it gave us Slumb'ring on a mother's breast.
Where the red cross fond-ly streaming, Flaps a - bove the frig-ate's deck,
Lo, the youth, be - come her lead - er! All her baf - fled ty - rants yield;
See the throne-less conqueror seat - ed, Rul - er by a peo - ple's choice;
List - en not to i - dle questions If its bands may be un - tied;
Gath -'ring while this ho - ly morn-ing Lights the land from sea to sea,

For the arm he stretched to save us, Be its morn for - ev - er blest.
Where the gold - en lil - ies, gleam-ing, Star the watchtow'rs of Que-bec.
Through his arm the Lord hath freed her; Crown him on the tent-ed field!
See the Pa - triot's task com-plet - ed, Hear the Fa- ther's dy - ing voice!
Doubt the pa - triot whose sug-ges-tions Strive a na - tion to di - vide!"
Hear thy coun -sel, heed thy warn-ing; Trust us, while we hon-or thee!

THE SWORD OF BUNKER HILL.

William Ross Wallace.
Moderato.

Bernard Covert.

1. He lay up - on his dy - ing bed; His eye was growing
2. The sword was brought, the sol-dier's eye Lit with a sud - den
3. "'Twas on that dread, im - mor-tal day, I dared the Brit-on's
4. "O, keep the sword"— his ac - cents broke— A smile — and he was

dim, When with a fee - ble voice he called His
flame; And as he grasped the an - cient blade, He
band, A cap - tain raised this blade on me,— I
dead— But his wrin - kled hand still grasped the blade Up -

weeping son to him: "Weep not, my boy!" the vet-'ran said, "I
murmered War-ren's name: Then said, "My boy, I leave you gold — But
tore it from his hand: And while the glo - rious bat - tle raged, It
on that dy - ing bed. The son re-mains; the sword re-mains — Its

bow   to Heav'n's high will— But quickly from   yon ant-lers bring The
what   is rich-er still,   I   leave you, mark   me, mark me now—. The
light-ened freedom's will— For, boy, The God   of freedom blessed The
glo-ry grow-ing still— And twen-ty mil - lions bless the sire, And

Sword   of   Bun-ker   Hill;   But quick-ly from   yon
Sword   of   Bun-ker   Hill;   I   leave you, mark   me,
Sword   of   Bun-ker   Hill;   For, boy, the God   of .
Sword   of   Bun-ker   Hill;   And twen-ty mil -   lions

ant - lers   bring   The   Sword   of   Bun - ker   Hill."
mark me   now—   The   Sword   of   Bun - ker   Hill."
free - dom   blessed   The   Sword   of   Bun - ker   Hill."
bless the   sire,   And   Sword   of   Bun - ker   Hill."

SONG OF THE NEGRO BOATMAN.

John Greenleaf Whittier.   Wenzel Müller.

Allegretto.

1. O,   praise an' tanks! de   Lord He come To   set de peo-ple
2. Ole   mas-sa   on he   trab-bels gone; He   leaf de land be-
3. We   pray de   Lord: He   gib us signs Dat   some day we be
4. We   know de   prom-ise   neb-ber fail, An'   neb-ber lie de

free;   An'   mas-sa tink it day ob doom, An'
blind: De   Lord's breff blow him fur-der on, Like
free;   De   norf-wind tell it to de pines, De
word;   So   like de 'pos-tles in de jail, We

we   ob   ju-bi-lee.   De Lord dat heap de
corn-shuck in   de   wind.   We own de hoe, we
wild-duck to   the   sea;   We tink it when de
wait-ed for   de   Lord: An' now He o-pen

Red Sea waves He jus' as 'trong as den: He
own de plough, We own de hands dat hold; We
church bell ring, We dream it in de dream; De
eb - 'ry door, An' trow a - way de key; He

say de word: We las' night slaves, To- day de Lord's free men.
sell de pig, We sell de cow, But neb - ber chile be sold.
rice - bird mean it when he sing, De ea - gle when he scream.
tink we lub Him so be - fore, We lub Him bet - ter free.

Chorus for each verse.

{ De yam will grow, de cot - ton blow, We'll hab de rice an' corn; }
{ O neb-ber you fear, if neb-ber you hear De dri - ver blow his horn! }

Sung at Christmas by the scholars of St. Helena's Island, S. C.

John Greenleaf Whittier.   Albert Gottlieb Methfessel.

Maestoso.

1. O none in all the world be - fore Were
2. Thou Friend and Help - er of the poor, Who
3. Bend low Thy pity - ing face and mild, And
4. We hear no more the driv - er's horn, No
5. The ver - y oaks are green - er clad, The
6. We praise Thee in our songs to - day, To
7. Come once A - gain, O bless - ed Lord! Come

ev - er glad as we! . . We're free on Car - o -
suf - fered for our sake, . . To o - pen ev - 'ry
help us sing and pray; . . The hand that blessed the
more the whip we fear, . . This ho - ly day that
wa - ters bright - er smile; . . O nev - er shone a
Thee in prayer we call, . . Make swift the feet and
walk - ing on the sea! . . And let the main - lands

li - na's shore, We're all . . . at home and free.
pris - on door, And ev - 'ry yoke to break!
lit - tle child, Up - on . . . our fore - heads lay.
saw Thee born Was nev - er half so dear.
day so glad On sweet . . St. Hel - en's Isle.
straight the way Of free - dom un - to all.
hear the word That sets . . . the is - lands free!

Thomas Buchanan Read.

William F. Hartley.

Martial style.

1. Where sweeps round the moun - tains the cloud on the
2. I mount the wild horse with no sad - dle or
3. When A - pril is sound - ing his horn o'er the

gale, And streams from their foun - tains leap in - to the
rein, And guide his swift course with a grasp on his
hills, And brook - lets are bound-ing in joy to the

vale,— As fright - ened deer leap when the storm with his
mane; Thro' paths steep and nar - row, and scorn - ing the
mills,— When warm Au - gust slum - bers a - mong her green

pack Rides o - ver the steep In the wild tor - rent's
crag, I chase with my ar - row the flight of the
leaves, And Har - vest en - cum - bers her gar - ners with

track,— Ev'n there my free home is; there watch I the
stag; Through snow - drifts en - gulf - ing, I fol - low the
sheaves, When the flail of No - vem - ber is swing-ing with

flocks Wan - der white as the foam Is on
bear, And face the gaunt wolf when he
might, And the mil - ler De - cem - ber is

stair - ways   of   rocks ;   Se - cure   in   the
snarls   in   his   lair,   And   watch   through the
man - tled   with white,—   In   field   and   in

gorge   there   in   free - dom   we   sing,   And
gorge   there   the   red   pan - ther   spring,   And
forge   there   the   free - heart - ed   sing,   And

laugh   at   King George, where   the   Ea - gle   is   king.

P. P. Bliss.   P. P. Bliss.

1. Let oth - ers sing of days gone by, O'er "good old times" let them
2. No voice have we for songs of yore, No thrones for kings who re -

grieve and sigh; Be ours a cheer-i - er, hap-pi - er lay, In
turn no more, But hail with spir - its so glad and so gay, The

praise of beau-ti - ful, wel - come To - day. To - day, . . . To -
songs and scenes that in - vite us to - day. To - day, . . . To -

O beau-ti - ful, welcome To -

day, The bright To - day; To - day, . . . To -
dry, The bright To - day; To - day, ... To -

day, To-day; The beau - ti - ful, bright To - day; O beau-ti - ful, wel-come To -

day; The bright To - day. With friends so true,
day; The bright To - day. With friends so true,

day, To-day; The beau-ti -ful, bright To - day. With friends so true, ... And

And pleasures new. La, la, la, la, la, la, la, la, la,
And pleasures new. La, la, la, la, la, la, la, la, la.

pleas-ures new . . . .

La, la, la, la, la, la, la, la, la, la, la, la, la, la,
La, la, la, la, la, la, la, la, la, la, la, la, la, la,

La, la, la, la, la, la, la, la, la, la, la. . . . .
La, la, la, la, la, la, la, la, la, la, la. . . . .

La, la, la, la.

LAUS DEO !

John Greenleaf Whittier.   Arr. from Jonathan Battishill.

1. It is done! Clang of bells and roar of gun
2. Ring, O bells! Every stroke ex - ult - ing tells
3. It is done! In the circuit of the sun
4. Ring and swing, Bells of joy! On morn - ing's wing

Send the ti - dings up and down;
Of the buri - al hour of crime;
Shall the sound there - of go forth;
Send the song of praise a - broad!

How the belfries rock and reel!
Loud and long that all may hear,
It shall bid the sad re - joice,
With a sound of bro - ken chains

How the great guns, peal on peal, Flug the joy from town to town!
Ring for every listening ear of E - ter - ni - ty and Time!
It shall give the dumb a voice, It shall belt with joy the earth!
Tell the nations that He reigns, Who a - lone is Lord and God!

Stephen Collins Foster.   **Stephen Collins Foster.**

1. { Way down up-on the Swa-nee rib-ber, Far, far a-way,
   { All up and down de whole cre-a-tion, Sad-ly I roam,
2. { All round de lit-tle farm I wan-dered When I was young,
   { When I was play-ing with my brudder, Hap-py was I,
3. { One lit-tle hut a-mong de bush-es, One dat I love,
   { When shall I hear de bees a-hum-ming All round de comb?

Dere's wha' my heart is turn-ing eb-er, Dere's wha' de old folks stay. }
Still long-ing for de old plan-ta-tion, And for de old folks at home. }
Den man-y hap-py days I squan-der'd Man-y de songs I sung; }
Oh! take me to my kind old mud-der, Dere let me live and die. }
Still sad-ly to my mem-'ry rush-es, No mat-ter where I rove. }
When shall I hear de ban-jo tum-ming Down in my good old home? }

CHORUS.

All de world am sad and drea-ry, Eb-'ry-where I roam;

Oh! dar-kies, how my heart grows wea-ry, Far from de old folks at home.

READY.

Phoebe Cary.   Unknown.

1. Loaded with gal - lant sol - diers, A boat shot in - to the land,
2. Low in the boat then each man lay, But quick the cap - tain said:
3. Firmly he rose, and fear-less-ly Stepped out in - to the tide;

And lay at the right of Rod - man's Point, With her
"If we lie here we are cap - tured all, And the
He pushed the ves - sel safe - ly off, Then

keel up - on the sand. Light - ly, gay-ly, they came to shore, And
first who moves is dead!" Then out- spoke a ne - gro sailor, No
fell a - cross her side: Pierced by ma-ny a ball he fell— The

nev - er a man a - fraid, When sud - den the en - e - my
slav - ish soul had he: "Somebod - y's got to
boat swung clear and free· But nev - er a man of

o - pened fire, From his dead - ly am - bus - cade.
die, boys, And it might as well be me!"
them that day Was fit - ter to die than he!

BATTLE HYMN OF THE REPUBLIC.

Julia Ward Howe.

Unknown.
(Air: John Brown's Body.)

1. Mine eyes have seen the glo - ry of the com - ing of the
2. I have seen him in the watch-fires of a hun - dred cir - cling
3. I have read a fie - ry gos - pel, writ in bur - nish'd rows of
4. He has sounded forth the trum - pet that shall nev - er call re -
5. In the beau - ty of the lil - ies Christ was born a - cross the

Lord; He is tramp-ling out the vint - age where the
camps; They have build - ed him an al - tar in the
steel; "As ye deal with my con - tem - ners, so with
treat; He is sift - ing out the hearts of men be -
sea, With a glo - ry in his bo - som that trans -

grapes of wrath are stored, He hath loosed the fate - ful light-ning of his
eve - ning dews and damps, I have read his right-eous sen - tence by the
you my grace shall deal: Let the he - ro born of wom-an crush the
fore his judg - ment-seat; Oh be swift, my soul, to an-swer him,—be
fig - ures you and me: As he died to make men ho - ly, let us

ter - ri - ble swift sword; His truth is march-ing on.
dim and flar - ing lamps; His day is march-ing on.
ser - pent with his heel, Since God is march-ing on.
ju - bi - lant, my feet! Our God is march-ing on.
die to make men free, While God is march-ing on.

Chorus.

Glo - ry! glo - ry! Hal - le - lu - jah! Glo - ry! glo - ry! Hal - le -

lu - jah! Glo - ry! glo - ry! Hal-le - lu - jah! His truth is march-ing on.

THE SWEET LITTLE MAN.

Dedicated to the Stay-at-home Rangers.

Oliver Wendell Holmes.

Scotch Air.
(Air: Bonnie Dundee.)

Moderato.

1. All the brave boys un - der can - vas are sleep - ing,
2. Bring him the but - ton - less gar - ment of wo - man!
3. All the fair maid - ens a - bout him shall clus - ter,
4. Now then, nine cheers for the Stay - at - home Ran - ger!

All of them press - ing to march with the van,
Cov - er his face lest it frec - kle and tan;
Pluck the white feath - ers from bon - net and fan,
Blow the great fish - horn and beat the big pan!

Far from the home where their sweet-hearts are weep - ing;
Mus - ter the A - pron - string Guards on the Com - mon,
Make him a plume like a tur - key - wing dus - ter,—
First in the field that is far - thest from dan - ger,

What are you wait - ing for, sweet lit - tle man?
That is the corps for the sweet lit - tle man!
That is the crest for the sweet lit - tle man!
Take your white-feath - er plume, sweet lit - tle man!

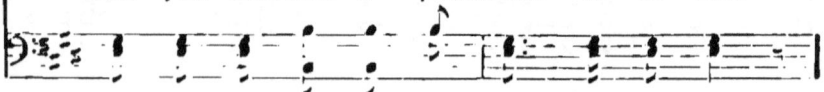

Sweet lit - tle man, O sweet lit - tle man;

What are you wait - ing for, sweet lit - tle man?

All the brave boys un - der can - vas are sleep - ing,—

What are you wait - ing for, sweet lit - tle man?

OUR COUNTRY.

John Greenleaf Whittier.   Arr. from Felix Mendelssohn-Bartholdy.

Maestoso.

1. We give thy na - tal day to hope, O
2. Thy pledge of freed - dom moves the world, And
3. Great, with - out seek - ing to be great By

coun - try of our love and prayer! Thy way is
all who hear it turn to thee, And read up -
fraud or con - quest; rich in gold, But rich - er

down no fa - tal slope, But up to free - er sun and air.
on thy flag un - furled The proph - e - cies of des - ti - ny.
In the large es - tate Of vir - tue which thy chil - dren hold;

mp   *cres.*

The fa - thers sleep, but men re - main, As wise, as true, and brave as
Thy great world-les - son all shall learn, The na - tions in thy school shall
With peace that comes of pu - ri - ty, And strength to sim - ple jus - tice

mp   *cres.*

they; Why count the loss and not the gain? The
sit, Earth's far - thest moun - tain - tops shall buru With
due, So runs our loy - al dream of thee; God

best is that we have to - day. O Land of lands! to thee we
watch-fires from thy own up - lit. O Land of lands! to thee we
of our fa - thers! make it true. O Land of lands! to thee we

give Our prayers, our hopes, our ser - vice free; For thee thy

sons shall no - bly live, And at thy need shall die for thee!

TENTING ON THE OLD CAMP-GROUND.

Walter Kittredge.   Walter Kittredge.

Tenderly.

1. We're tent - ing to - night on the old Camp - ground;
2. We're tent - ing to - night on the old Camp - ground,
3. We are tired of war on the old Camp - ground;
4. We've been fight - ing to - day on the old Camp - ground;

Give us a song to cheer Our wea - ry hearts, a
Think - ing of days gone by, Of the loved ones at home that
Man - y are dead and gone Of the brave and true who've
Man - y are ly - ing near; Some are dead, and

song of home, And friends we love so dear.
gave us the hand, And the tear that said "good - bye!"
left their homes, Oth - ers been wound-ed long.
some are dying, Man-y the fall - ing tear.

CHORUS.

Man - y are the hearts that are wea - ry to - night,

Wish - ing for the war to cease; Man - y are the hearts

look - ing for the right, To see the dawn of peace.

pp

Vs.1.2.3. Tenting to-night, tent-ing to-night, Tent-ing on the old Camp-ground.
Vs.4. Dy - ing to-night, dy - ing to-night, Dy - ing on the old Camp-ground.

pp

DECORATION DAY.

Henry Wadsworth Longfellow. Johann Aegidius Geyer.

1. Sleep, comrades, sleep, sleep and rest On this Field of the
2. Rest, comrades, rest, rest and sleep! The thoughts of men shall
3. Your si - lent tents, tents of green, We deck with flowers, with

p

Ground - ed Arms, Where foes no more molest, Nor sen-try's shot a - larms!
ev - er be As sen - ti - nels to keep Your rest from danger free.
fra - grant flow'rs; Yours has the suf-f'ring been, The mem'ry shall be ours,

p

Sleep, com-rades, sleep and rest On this Field of the Grounded Arms.
As sen - ti - nels to keep Your rest from dan - ger free.
Yours has the suf - 'ring been, The mem-'ry shall be ours.

THE FLAG.

James Riley.

L. V. H. Crosby.
(Air: Dearest Mae.)

1. That o - cean-guarded flag of light, for - ev - er may it fly! It
2. Timbers have crash'd and guns have peal'd be - neath its ar - dent glow; But
3. Its stripes of red, e - ter - nal dyed with heart-streams of all lands; Its

flashed o'er Monmouth's bloody fight, and lit Mc - Hen-ry's sky; It
nev - er did that en - sign yield its hon - or to the foe; Its
white, the snow-capped hills that hide in storm their up - raised hands; Its

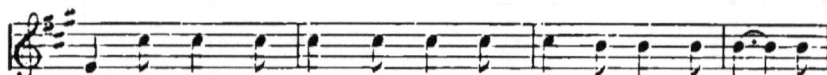

bears up - on its folds of flame to earth's re -mot - est wave The
fame shall march with mar - tial tread down a - ges yet to be To
blue, the o - cean waves that beat round freedom's cir - cled shore; Its

names of men whose deeds of fame shall e'er in - spire the brave.
guard those stars that nev - er paled in fight on land or sea.
stars, the prints of an - gels' feet, that shine for-ev - er more.

CHORUS.

For - ev - er may it fly! For - ev - er may it fly! That

o - cean-guarded flag of light, For - ev - er may it fly!

John Greenleaf Whittier. John Knowles Paine.

Maestoso.

1. Our fathers' God, from out whose hand The cen-turies fall like grains
2. Here, where of old by Thy de - sign, The fa - thers spake that word
3. For art and la - bor met in truce, For beau-ty made the bride
4. Oh make Thou us, thro' cen-turies long, In peace se - cure, in jus -

of sand, We meet to - day, u - nit - ed, free, And
of Thine Whose ech - o is the glad re - frain Of
of use, We thank Thee; but, with - al, we crave The
tice strong; A - round our gift of free - dom draw The

loy - al to our land and Thee, To thank Thee for the
rend - ed bolt and fall - ing chain, To grace our fes - tal
au - stere vir - tues strong to save, The hon - or proof to
safe-guards of Thy right - eous law; And, cast in some di -

e - ra done, And trust Thee for the o - p'ning one.
time, from all The zones of earth, our guests we call.
place or gold, The man - hood nev - er bought nor sold!
vin - er mould, Let the new cy - cle shame the old!

O CAPTAIN! MY CAPTAIN!

Walt Whitman.   Arr. from O. M. Wyman.

O Captain! my Captain! our fearful trip is done,
O Captain! my Captain! rise up and hear the bells;
My Captain does not answer, his lips are pale and still;

The ship has weathered every rack, the prize we sought is won;
Rise up,— for you the flag is flung — for you the bu - gle trills;
My father does not feel my arm, he has no pulse nor will;

The port is near, the bells I hear, the people all ex - ult - ing,
For you bouquets and ribbon'd wreaths — for you the shores a - crowd-ing,
The ship is anchor'd safe and sound, its voyage closed and done;

While follow eyes the steady keel, the ves - sel
For you they call, the swaying mass — their ea - ger
From fearful trip the victor ship comes in with

grim and dar - ing;   But O heart!   heart!   heart!
fa - ces turn - ing;   Here Captain!   dear   father!
ob - ject won: Exult, O shores, and   ring, O   bells!

O the bleeding drops of red,   Where on the deck my Captain lies,
This arm be - neath your head!   It is some dream that on the deck You've
But I walk with mournful tread,   Walk the deck my Captain lies,

3d stanza only.

Fall - en cold and dead.
fall - en cold and dead.
Fall - en cold and dead.   Cold and dead.

COLUMBUS.

Joaquin Miller.

Unknown.
(A German Air.)

mf

1. Be - hind him lay the gray A - zores, Be - hind the gates of
2. "My men grow mut'- nous day by day; My men grow ghast-ly
3. They sailed and sailed, as winds might blow, Un - til at last the
4. They sailed, they sailed, then spoke his mate :"This mad sea shows his
5. Then, pale and worn, he kept his deck, And thro' the dark-ness

mf

Her - cu - les; Be - fore him not the ghost of shores, Be -
wau and weak." The stout mate tho't of home; a spray Of
blanch'd mate said; "Why, now, not e - ven God would know Should
teeth to - night, He curls his lip, he lies in wait, With
peered that night. Ah, dark - est night! and then a speck— A

fore him on - ly shore - less seas. The good mate said: "Now
salt wave wash'd his swar - thy cheek. "What shall I say, brave
I and all my men fall dead. These ver - y winds for -
lift - ed teeth as if to bite! Brave Ad - mi - ral, say
light! a light! a light! a - light! It grew—a star - lit

must we pray, For lo! the ver - y stars are gone; Speak,
Ad - mi - ral, If we sight naught but seas at dawn?" "Why,
get their way, For God from these dread seas is gone. Now
but one word; What shall we do when hope is gone?" The
flag un - furled! It grew to be Time's burst of dawn; He

Ad - mi - ral, what shall I say?" "Why say, sail on! and on!"
you shall say, at break of day: 'Sail on! sail on! and on!'"
speak, brave Ad - mi - ral, and say— He said: "Sail on! sail on! and on!"
words leaped as a leap - ing sword :"Sail on! sail on! and on!"
gained a world! he gave that world Its watch-word :"On! and on!"

Richard Henry Stoddard.

U. Munjinger.

Moderato.

1. When the sum - mer days are bright and long, And the
'T is sweet in the sha - dy wood to lie, And

2. When win - ter comes and the days are dim, And the
'T is sweet in the fad - ed woods to stray, And

3. Sum - mer or win - ter, day or night, The
They give us peace, and they make us strong, Such

lit - tle birds pipe a mer - ry song,
gaze at the leaves and the twink - ling sky,
wind is sing - ing a mourn - ful hymn,
tread the dead leaves In - to the clay,
woods are an ev - er new de - light;
won - der - ful balms to them be - long:

Drink - ing the while the rare, cool breeze,
Think - ing of all life's mys - ter - ies. . .
So, liv - ing or dy - ing, I'll take mine ease . .

Un - der the trees, ... un - der the trees.

THE STORM SONG.

Bayard Taylor.

Arr. from Christoph Willibald Gluck.

1. The clouds are scud - ding a - cross the moon, A
2. Broth - ers, a night of ter - ror and gloom Speaks
3. Down with the hatch - es on those who sleep! The
4. Tho' the rig - ging shriek In his might-y grip, And the
5. Yet, cour - age, broth - ers! we trust the wave, With

mist - y light is on the sea; The
in the cloud and gath-'ring roar, Thank
wild and whis - tling deck have we; Good
na - ked spars be snapped a - way, Lashed
God a - bove, our guid-ing chart: So,

wind | in | the | shrouds | has a | win - try tune, | And the
God, | He has | giv'n | us | broad sea - room, | A
watch, | my | brothers, | to - | night we'll keep, | While the
to | the | helm, | we'll | drive our ship | In the
whether | to | har - bor | or | o - cean-grave, | Be it

foam | is | fly - ing | free, ... | And the
thou - | sand | miles | from | shore, ... | A
tem - pest | is | on | the | sea, ... | While the
teeth of | the | whelm - ing | spray, ... | In the
still | with a | cheer - y | heart, ... | Be it

foam . . | is | fly - | ing | free.
thou - | sand | miles | from | shore.
tem - | pest is | on | the | sea!
teeth | of the | whelm - | ing | spray!
still | with a | cheer - | y | heart!

THE FISHERMEN.

John Greenleaf Whittier.   Christian Gottlob Neefe.

1. Hur - rah! the sea - ward breez - es   Sweep down the bay a - main;
2. We'll drop our lines, and gath - er   Old o - cean's treas-ures in,
3. Tho' the mist up-on   our   jack - ets   In the bit - ter air con-geals,
4. Hur - rah! hur-rah! the west - wind Comes fresh-'ning down the bay,

Heave up, my lads, the an - chor! Run   up   the sail a - gain!
Wher-e'er   the   mot - tled mackerel   Turns up   a   steel-dark fin;
And our lines wind stiff and slow - ly   From off the fro - zen reels;
The   ris - ing sails are fill - ing,—Give way, my lads, give way!

Leave   to   the lub - ber lands-men   The   rail - car and the steed;
The   sea's our field of   har - vest, Its   scal - y   tribes our grain;
Tho' the fog be thick a - round us And the storm blow high and loud,
Leave the cow- ard lands-man cling - ing To the dull earth, like a weed,

The stars of heav'n shall guide us, The breath of heav'n shall speed.
We'll reap the teem - ing wa - ters As at home they reap the plain!
We'll whis - tle down the wild wind, And laugh be - neath the cloud!
The stars of heav'n shall guide us, The breath of heav'n shall speed!

THE VOYAGERS.

Bayard Taylor.

Friedrich Silcher.
(Air: Die Lorelei.)

Moderato.

1. No long-er spread the sail! No long-er strain the oar!
2. Each morn we see its peaks, Made beau-ti-ful with snow;
3. And still the keel is swift, And still the wind is free,
4. O shipmates, leave the ropes, And what tho' no one steers,

For nev-er yet has blown the gale Will bring us near-er shore.
Each eve its vales and wind-ing creeks, That sleep in mist be-low.
And still as far its moun-tains lift Be-yond th' en-chanted sea.
We sail no fast-er for our hopes, No slow-er for our fears.

The sway-ing keel slides on, The helm o-beys the hand;
At noon we mark the gleam Of tem-ples tall and fair;
Yet vain is all re-turn, Though false the goal be-fore;
How-e'er the bark is blown, Lie down and sleep a-while:

Fast we have sailed from dawn to dawn, Yet nev-er reach the land.
At mid-night watch its bon-fires stream In the au-ro-ral air.
The gale is ev-er dead a-stern, The cur-rent sets to shore.
What prof-its toil, when chance a-lone Can bring us to the Isle?

THE HUNTER'S SERENADE.

William Cullen Bryant.   German Air.

Affettuoso.

1. Thy bow'r is fin - ished, fair - est! Fit bow'r for hun - ter's bride,
2. For thee the wild-grape glist - ens On sun - ny knoll and tree,
3. Come, thou hast not for - got - ten Thy pledge and prom-ise quite,

Where old woods o - ver - shad - ow The green sa - van - na's side.
The slim pa - pa - ya ri - pens Its yel - low fruit for thee.
With ma - ny blushes mur - mered, Be - neath the even - ing light.

I've wan - der'd long, and wandered far, And nev - er have I met, . .
For thee the duck, on glass-y stream, The prai - rie-fowl shall die; . .
Then come, the vio - lets crowd my door, Thy ear - liest look to win, . .

In all this love-ly West-ern land, A spot so love-ly yet;
My ri-fle for thy feast shall bring The wild-swan from the sky.
And at my si-lent win-dow-sill The jes-sa-mine peeps in.

mf ... *p*

But I shall think it fair-er When thou art come to bless,
The for-est's leap-ing pan-ther, Fierce, beauti-ful and fleet,
All day the red-bird war-bles Up-on the mulber-ry near,

With thy sweet smile and sil-ver voice, Its si-lent love-li-ness.
Shall yield his spot-ted hide to be A car-pet for thy feet.
And the night-spar-row trills her song All night, with none to hear.

WIND AND SEA.

Bayard Taylor.

Johann A. P. Schulz.

1. The Sea is a jo-vial com-rade, He laughs wher-ev-er he
2. But the Wind is sad and rest-less, And cursed with an in-ward
3. Wel-come are both their vol-ces, And I know not which is

goes; His mer-ri-ment shines in the
pain; You may hark as you will, by
best,— The laugh-ter that slips from the

dimp-ling lines That wrin-kle his hale re-pose;
val-ley or hill, But you hear him still com-plain.
O-cean's lips, Or the com-fort-less Wind's un-rest.

Solo.

He lays him-self down at the feet of the sun,
He walls on the bar-ren moun-tains,
There's a pang in all re-joic-ing.

And shakes all o - ver with glee, . .
And shrieks on the win - try sea; . .
A joy in the heart of pain, . .

Chorus

And the broad-backed bil - lows fall faint on the shore, In the
He sobs in the ce - dar, and moans in the pine, And
And the Wind that sad - dens, the Sea that glad-dens, Are

mirth of the might - y, might - y Sea!
shudders all o - ver the as - pen tree.
sing - ing, are sing-ing the self - same strain!

A LIFE ON THE OCEAN WAVE.

Epes Sargent.

Henry Russell.

1. A life on the o - cean wave, A home on the roll-ing
2. Once more on the deck I stand Of my own swift-glid-ing
3. The land is no longer in view, The clouds have be - gun to

deep, Where the scat - tered wa - ters rave, And the
craft, Set sail! fare - well to the land, The
frown, But with a stout ves- sel and crew We'll

FINE.   mp

winds their rev - els keep: Like an ea - gle . caged I
gale fol-lows far a - baft: We shoot thro' the spark - ling
say "Let the storm come down!" And the song of our heart shall

mp

pine On this dull, un - chang - ing shore: Oh!
foam, Like an o - cean bird set free; Like the
be, While the winds and the wa - ters rave, A

Agitato.

Sing first verse in D. C.

give me the flash - ing brine, The spray and the tem - pest roar!
o - cean bird, our home We'll find far out on the sea!
life on the heav - ing sea, A home on the bound - ing wave!

John Greenleaf Whittier.   Johann André.

Maestoso.

1. Once more the lib - 'ral year laughs out . . O'er
2. Our com - mon moth - er rests and sings, . Like
3. O fa - vors ev - 'ry year made new! . . O
4. We shut our eyes, the flowers bloom on; . . We
5. So let these al - tars wreathed with flowers . And

rich - er stores than gems or gold; Once more with har - vest
Ruth, a - mong her gar-nered sheaves; Her lap is full of
gifts with rain and sun - shine sent! The boun-ty o - ver-
mur - mur, but the corn - ears fill; We choose the shad - ow,
piled with fruits, a - wake a - gain Thanksgiv-ings for the

song and shout Is Na - ture's blood - less tri - umph
good - ly things, Her brow is bright with au - tumn
runs our due, The full - ness shames our dis - con -
but the sun That casts it shines be - hind us
gold - en hours, The ear - ly and the lat - ter

told, With song and shout is Nature's bloodless tri - umph told.
leaves, Her lap is full, her brow is bright with Au - tumn leaves.
tent, The full - ness o - ver - runs our due, and shames our dis-con-tent.
still, We choose the shad - ow, but the sun is shin - ing still.
rain! The gold-en hours, the ear - ly and the lat - ter rain!

THE CORN SONG.

John Greenleaf Whittier.

German Air.

Allegretto.

1. Heap high the farm-er's win - try hoard! Heap high the gold-en corn!
2. Let oth - er lands,ex - ult - ing,glean The ap - ple from the pine,
3. Thro' vales of grass and meads of flow'rs Our ploughs their furrows made,
4. All thro' the long,bright days of June Its leaves grew green and fair,
5. Let vap - id i - dlers loll in silk A - round their cost-ly board;

No rich - er gift has Au - tumn poured From out her lav - ish horn!
The or - ange from its glossy green, The clus - ter from the vine;
While on the hills the sun and showers Of changeful A - pril played.
And wav'd in hot mid-sum-mer's noon Its soft and yel - low hair.
Give us the bowl of samp and milk, By home-spun beau-ty poured!

So let the good old crop a - dorn The hills our fa - thers trod;
We bet - ter love the har - dy gift Our rug - ged vales be - stow,
We dropp'd the seed o'er hill and plain, Be - neath the sun of May,
And now, with au-tumn's moon-lit eves, Its har - vest-time has come,
Where'er the wide old kitch - en hearth Sends up its smoky curls,

Still let us, for his gold-en corn, Send up our thanks to God!
To cheer us when the storm shall drift Our har-vest-fields with snow.
And frighten'd from our sprouting grain The rob-ber crows a - way.
We pluck a - way the frost-ed leaves, And bear the treas-ure home.
Who will not thank the kind-ly earth, And bless our farm-er girls!

THE RAVEN.

Edgar Allan Poe.

1. Once upon a midnight dreary, while I pondered, weak and weary, Over many a quaint and curious volume of for-got-ten lore;

While I nodded, nearly napping, suddenly there came a tapping, as of some one gently rapping, rapping at my cham-ber door;

"'T is some visitor," I muttered, "tapping at my chamber door; Only this and noth-ing more."

2. Ah, distinctly I remember, it was in the bleak December,
   And each separate dying ember wrought its | ghost upon the | floor; ||
   Eagerly I wished the morrow, vainly I had sought to borrow
   From my books surcease of sorrow, sorrow | for the lost Le- | nore; ||
   For the rare and radiant maiden, | whom the angels | name Lenore, ||
   Nameless | here, for ever- | more. ||

3. Open then I flung the shutter, when, with many a flirt and flutter,
   In there stepped a stately raven of the | sainted days of | yore. ||
   Not the least obeisance made he; not an instant stopped or staid he;
   But, with mien of lord or lady, perched a- | bove my chamber | door; ||
   Perched upon a bust of Pallas, just a- | bove my chamber | door; ||
   Perched and | sat, and nothing | more. ||

4. And the raven, never flitting, still is sitting — still is sitting
   On the pallid bust of Pallas, just a- | bove my chamber | door : ||
   And his eyes have all the seeming of a demon that is dreaming,
   And the lamplight o'er him streaming throws his | shadow on the | floor; ||
   And my soul from out that shadow, that lies | floating on the | floor, ||
   Shall be | lifted — never | more." ||

HOME, SWEET HOME.

John Howard Payne.   Sicilian Air.

1. {Mid pleas-ures and pal-a-ces though we may roam,
Be it ev-er so hum-ble, there's no place (*Omit.* . . .)
2. {An ex-ile from home, splendor daz-zles in vain;
Oh! give me my low-ly thatch'd cot-tage (*Omit.* . . .)

like home; } . {A charm from the skies seems to
Which, seek thro' the world, is ne'er
The birds sing-ing gai-ly, that
a-gain; } {Give me these, with the peace of mind

hal-low us there, *Omit.* . } Home, home,—sweet, sweet home! There's
met with (*Omit.* .) else-where; }
came at my call—
dear-er (*Omit.* .) than all. }

no place like home, There's no place like home.

3 How sweet 't is to sit 'neath a fond father's smile,
And the cares of a mother to soothe and beguile.
Let others delight 'mid new pleasures to roam,
But give me, oh! give me the pleasures of home!
REFRAIN.

4 To thee I'll return, overburdened with care,
The heart's dearest solace will smile on me there.
No more from that cottage again will I roam,
Be it ever so humble, there's no place like home.
REFRAIN.

Marshall S. Pike.
Two or four parts.

Marshall S. Pike.

1. Home a - gain, home a - gain, From a for - eign shore! And
2. Hap - py hearts, hap - py hearts, With mine have laughed in glee, And
3. Mu - sic sweet, mu - sic soft, Ling - ers round the place, And

FINE.

oh, it fills my soul with joy. To meet my friends once more.
oh, the friends I loved in youth, Seem hap - pi - er to me;
oh, I feel the child - hood charm That time can - not ef - face.

pp

Here I dropped the part - ing tear, To cross the o - cean's foam,
And if my guide should be the fate, Which bids me long - er roam,
Then give me but my homestead roof, I'll ask no pal - ace dome,

pp

1st stanza in D.C.

But now I'm once a - gain with those Who kind - ly greet me home.
But death a - lone can break the tie That binds my heart to home.
For I can live a hap - py life With those I love at home.

D.C.

AROUND THE HEARTH.

George Howland.

Scotch Air.
(Air: Auld Lang Syne.)

Andante.

1. What-ev - er be our earth-ly lot, Wher-ev - er we may roam, Still
2. When win- ter, com-ing in its wrath, Pil'd high the drifting snow, Safe
3. When wea-ried with our ea - ger chase, Thro' many a tangled path, How
4. And brighter with the pass - ing years Seems childhood's sweet employ, And

to our hearts the bright-est spot Is round the hearth at home. The
clus - ter'd round the cheer- ful hearth, We watch'd the fire - light glow; Nor
sweet the dear ac - cus - tom'd place To take a - round the hearth! And
ev - er sweet-er still ap - pears Each well - re - mem - ber'd joy, A -

home that wel - comed us at birth, The hearth by which we sat; No
bright-er seem'd the rud - dy flames Than did our hearts, the while A
still when by our toil and care We feel our-selves op - press'd, Our
round the cheer-ful hearth at home, Where we in child - hood sat; No

oth - er spot on all the earth Will ev - er be like that.
lov - ing moth-er breath'd our names With sweet ap - prov- ing smile.
thoughts forev - er clus - ter there, And there a - lone find rest.
oth - er spot, wher-e'er we roam, Will ev - er be like that.

Lucy Larcom.
Alleyretto.

German Air.

mf

1. If I were a sun - beam, I know what I'd do;
2. If I were a sun - beam, I know where I'd go;
3. Art thou not a sun - beam, Child whose life is glad

cres. *dim.*

I would seek white lil - ies The rain - y wood - land through.
In - to low - liest hov - els, Dark with want and woe;
With an in - ner ra - diance Sun - shine nev - er had?

I would steal a - mong them, Soft - est light I'd shed,
Till sad hearts look'd up - ward, I would shine and shine;
O, as God hath bless'd thee, Scat - ter rays di - vine!

f

Un - til ev - 'ry lil - y Raised its droop-ing head.
Then they'd think of heav - en, Their sweet home and mine.
For there is no sun - beam But must die or shine.

A MIDSUMMER SONG.

Richard Watson Gilder.

Franz Abt.

Allegretto.

1. Oh fa-ther's gone to mark-et-town he was up be-fore the day,
2. From all the mist-y morn-ing air there comes a - sum-mer sound.
3. A-bove the trees the hon-ey bees swarm by with buzz and boom,
4. How strange at such a time of day the mill should stop its clatter!

And Ja-mie's aft-er rob-ins, and the man is mak-ing hay,
A murmur as of wa-ters, from skies and trees and ground.
And in the field and gar-den a thousand blos-soms bloom;
The farm-er's wife is listen-ing now, and won-ders what's the matter.

And whistling down the hol-low goes the boy who minds the mill,
The birds they sing up-on the wing, the pig-eons bill and coo;
Within the far-mer's mead-ow, a brown-eyed dais-y blows.
Oh, wild the birds are sing-ing in the wood and on the hill,

While moth-er from the kitchen door is call-ing with a will,
And o-ver hill and hol-low rings a-gain the loud hal-loo:
And down at the edge of the hol-low a red and thorn-y rose.
While whist-ling up the hol-low goes the boy that minds the mill.

Pol - ly!   Pol - ly!

Oh, Pol - ly! the cows are in the corn!   Oh,   where's Pol - ly?

GOD SPEED THE RIGHT.

W. E. Hickson.   German Air.

Maestoso.

1. { Now to heav'n our pray'r as - cend - ing, God speed the right; }
   { In a no - ble cause con - tend - ing, God speed the right; }

2. { Be that pray'r a - gain re - peat - ed, God speed the right; }
   { Ne'er de - spair - ing, tho' de - feat - ed, God speed the right; }

3. { Pa - tient, firm, and per - se - ver - ing, God speed the right; }
   { Ne'er th' event nor dan - ger fear - ing, God speed the right; }

Be our zeal in heav'n re - cord - ed, With suc - cess on
Like the good and great in sto - ry, If we fail we
Pains, nor toils, nor tri - als heed - ing, In the strength of

earth re - ward - ed, God speed the right, God speed the right.
fail with glo - ry, God speed the right, God speed the right.
heav'n suc - ceed - ing, God speed the right, God speed the right.

RAIN ON THE ROOF.

Coates Kinney.
Andantino.
Johann Gottlieb Naumann.

1. When the hu - mid show-ers gath-er O - ver all the star-ry spheres,
2. Ev - 'ry tin - kle on the shin-gles Has an ech-o in the heart,
3. There in fan - cy comes my moth-er, As she used to years a - gone,
4. Then my lit - tle ser - aph sis - ter, With her wings and wav-ing hair,
5. There is naught in art's bra-vur - as That can work with such a spell,

And the mel - an - chol - y dark-ness Gen - tly falls in rainy tears,
And a thou-sand dreamy fan - cies In - to bus - y be-ing start,
To sur - vey the in - fant sleepers, Ere she left them till the dawn.
And her bright-eye'd cher-ub - brother, A se-rene an - gel-ic pair,
In the spir - it's pure, deep fountains Whence the ho - ly passions swell,

'T is a joy to press the pil - low Of a cot - tage chamber bed,
And a thou-sand rec - ol - lec-tions Weave their bright hues in - to woof
I can see her bend-ing o'er me, As I list - en to the strain
Glide a - round my wake-ful pil - low, With their praise or mild re - proof,
As that mel - o - dy of na-ture, That sub-dued, sub - du - ing strain,

And to list - en to the pat - ter Of the soft rain o - ver-head.
As I list - en to the pat - ter Of the soft rain on the roof.
Which is play'd up - on the shin-gles By the pat - ter of the rain.
As I list - en to the mur-mur Of the soft rain on the roof.
Which is play'd up - on the shin-gles By the pat - ter of the rain.

George Pope Morris.

Johann Adam Hiller.

1. Woodman, spare that tree, Touch not a sin - gle bough!
2. That old fa - mil - iar tree, Whose glo - ry and re - nown
3. When but an I - dle boy, I sought its grate - ful shade;
4. My heart-strings round thee cling Close as thy bark, old friend;

In youth it shel - tered me, And I'll pro - tect it now.
Are spread o'er land and sea — And would'st thou hew it down?
In all their gush-ing joy Here, too, my sis - ters played.
Here shall the wild-bird sing, And still thy branch-es bend.

'Twas my fore - fa - ther's hand That placed it near his cot;
Wood-man, for - bear thy stroke, Cut not its earth - bound ties!
My mother kissed me here; My fa - ther press'd my hand —
Old tree, the storm still brave! And, wood - man, leave the spot;

Then, wood-man, let it stand, Thy axe shall harm it not.
Oh, spare that a - ged oak Now tow'r - ing to the skies!
For - give this fool - ish tear, But let the old oak stand.
While I've a hand to save, Thy axe shall harm it not.

THE OLD OAKEN BUCKET.

G. Kiallmark.
(Air: Araby's Daughter.)

Samuel Woodworth.

1. { How dear to this heart are the scenes of my child-hood, When
The or-chard, the mead-ow, the deep-tan-gled wild-wood, And

D.C. The old oak-en buck-et—the i-ron-bound buck-et—The

FINE

fond rec-ol-lec-tion pre-sents them to view!
ev-'ry loved spot which my in-fan-cy knew; }

moss-cov-ered buck-et which hung in the well.

The wide-spread-ing pond, and the mill that stood by it— The
The cot of my fath-er, the dai-ry-house nigh it. And

D.C.

bridge and the rock where the cat-a-ract fell—
e'en the rude buck-et which hung in the well. }

D.C.

2. That moss-covered vessel I hail as a treasure —
   For often, at noon, when returned from the field,
   I found it the source of an exquisite pleasure,
   The purest and sweetest that nature can yield;
   How ardent I seized it, with hands that were glowing,
   And quick to the white-pebbled bottom it fell —
   Then soon, with the emblem of truth overflowing,
   And dripping with coolness, it rose from the well —
   The old oaken bucket — the iron-bound bucket —
   The moss-covered bucket arose from the well.

3. How sweet from the green mossy brim to receive it,
   As poised on the curb, it inclined to my lips!
   Not a full-blushing goblet could tempt me to leave it,
   Though filled with the nectar that Jupiter sips.
   And now, far removed from the loved habitation,
   The tear of regret will intrusively swell,
   As fancy reverts to my father's plantation,
   And sighs for the bucket, which hangs in the well —
   The old oaken bucket — the iron-bound bucket —
   The moss-covered bucket which hangs in the well.

Isaac B. Woodbury.

Isaac B. Woodbury.

1. Speed a - way! speed a - way! on thine er - rand of light! There's a
2. And oh! wilt thou tell her, blest bird on the wing, That her
3. Go, bird of the sil - ver wing! fet - ter - less now; Stoop

young heart a - wait-ing thy com-ing to - night; She will fon-dle thee
moth-er hath ev - er a sad song to sing; That she standeth a -
not thy bright pin - ions on yon mountain's brow; But hie thee a -

close, she will ask for the lov'd, Who pine up - on earth since the
lone, in the still qui-et night, And her fond heart goes forth for the
way, o'er rock, riv - er and glen, And find our young "Day Star," ere

"Day Star" has roved, She will ask if we miss her, so long is her
be - ing of light, Who had slept in her bo - som,—but who would not
night close a - gain; Up, on - ward! let noth-ing thy mis - sion de -

stay.
stay?
lay.

Speed a - way! Speed a - way! Speed a - way!

THE INDIAN GIRL'S LAMENT.

William Cullen Bryant. Arr. from Felix Mendelssohn-Bartholdy.

Andante.   *p*

1. An In - dian girl was sit - ting where Her lov - er, slain in
2. "'Twas I the broid-ered moc - sen made, That shod thee for that
3. With wam-pum belts I cross'd thy breast, And wrapped thee in the
4. Thou'rt hap - py now, for thou hast passed The long dark jour - ney
5. Yet, oft to thine own In - dian maid Even there thy thoughts will

Andante.   *p*

cres.

bat - tle, slept; Her maid - en veil, her own black hair. Came
dis - tant land; 'Twas I thy bow and ar - rows laid Be -
bi - son's hide, And laid the food that pleased thee best In
of the grave, And in the land of light, at last, Hast
earth-ward stray— To her who sits where thou wert laid, And

cres.

dim.

down o'er eyes, o'er eyes that wept; And wild - ly, in her
side thy still, thy still cold hand; Thy bow in many a
plen - ty, plen - ty by thy side; And decked thee brave-ly
joined the good, the good and brave A - mid the flushed and
weeps the hours, the hours a - way, Yet al - most can her

dim.

This sad and sim - ple lay she sung. . . . .
Thy ar - rows nev - er vain - ly sent. . . . .
A war - rior of il - lus - trious name . . . . .
The brav - est and the love-liest there. . . . .
To think that thou dost love her yet. . . . .

dim.   *pp*

wood-land tongue, This sad and sim-ple, sim - ple lay she sung.
bat - tle bent, Thy ar - rows nev-er, nev - er vain - ly sent.
as be - came, A war - rior, war-rior of il - lus - trious name
balm-y air, The brav-est, bravest and the love - liest there.
grief for - get, To think that thou, that thou dost love her yet."

pp

YE SAY THEY ALL HAVE PASSED AWAY.

Lydia Huntley Sigourney.
Moderato.

Wellington Guernsey.
(Air: I'll hang my harp on a willow tree.)

1. Ye say they all have pass'd a - way, That no - ble race and brave,
2. 'Tis where On - ta - rio's bil - low Like o - cean's surge is curl'd,
3. Ye say their cone-like cab - ins That clus-ter'd o'er the vale,
4. Old Mas - sa - chusetts wears it With - in her lord-ly crown,
5. Wa-chu - sett hides its lin-g'ring voice With-in his rocky heart,

That their light ca - noes have van - ish'd From off the crest-ed wave.
Where strong Ni - ag-a-ra's thunders wake The ech - oes of the world,
Have dis - ap-pear'd, as wither'd leaves Be - fore the autumn gale;
And broad O - hi - o bears' it A - mid his young re - nown;
And Al - le - gha - ny graves its tone Thro'out his loft-y chart;

That, mid the for - ests where they roam'd, There rings no hun - ter's shout;
Where red Mis-sou - ri bring - eth Rich tri - bute from the west,
But their mem'ry liv - eth on your hills, Their bap - tism on your shore,
Con - nect-i - cut hath wreath'd it Where her qui - et foli - age waves,
Mo - nad-nock, on his fore-head hoar, Doth seal the sa - cred trust;

But their name is on your riv - ers, Ye may not wash it out.
And Rap - pa - han - nock sweetly sleeps On green Virgi - nia's breast.
Your ev - er - last-ing riv-ers speak Their di - a - lect of yore.
And bold Ken-tuck-y breathes it hoarse Thro' all her an - cient caves.
Your moun - tains build their mon-u-ments, Tho' ye destroy their dust.

MY MOTHER'S MEMORY.

John Boyle O'Reilly.   Wilhelm Taubert.

1. There is one bright star in heav - en, Ev - er shin - ing
2. In my far - thest, wild - est wan - d'rings I have turned me

In my night; God to me one guide has giv - en,
to that love, As a div - er 'neath the wa - ter,

Like the sai - lor's bea - con light, Set on ev - 'ry
Turns to watch the light a - bove,— There is one bright

shoal and dan - ger, Send - ing out its warn - ing ray To the
star in heav - en Ev - er shin - ing in my night; God to

home-bound, wea - ry stran - ger Looking for the land-locked bay.
me one guide has giv - en, Like the sai - lor's bea - con light.

Henry Wadsworth Longfellow.

Charles C. Converse.

Andantino.

1. In the wig - wam with No - ko - mis,
2. "No, my child!" said old No - ko - mis,
3. "No, my child!" said old No - ko - mis,

With those gloom - y guests that watched her,
"'Tis the night - wind in the pine - trees!" —
"'Tis the smoke, that waves and beck - ons!" —

With the fam - ine and the fev - er, She was ly - ing,
"No, my child!" said old No - ko - mis, "'Tis the night - wind
"No, my child!" said old No - ko - mis, "'Tis the smoke, that

Min - ne - ha - ha.
In   the   pine - trees!"
waves and   beck - ons!"

"Hark!"   she   said;   "I   hear   a   rush - ing,
"Look!"   she   said;   "I   see   my   fa - ther
"Ah!"   said   she,   "the   eyes   of   Pau - guk

Hear   a   roar - ing   and   a   rush - ing,
Stand - ing   lone - ly   at   his   door - way,
Glare   up - on   me   in   the   dark - ness,

Hear the Falls of Min - ne - ha - ha,
Beck - 'ning to me from his wig - wam
I can feel his i - cy fin - gers—

Call - ing to me from a dis - tance!"
In the land of the Da - co - tahs!"
Hi - a - wa - tha! Hi - a - wa - tha!"

4 And the des'late Hiawatha,
Far away amid the forest,
Heard the voice of Minnehaha
Calling to him in the darkness.
Over snow-fields waste and pathless,
Homeward hurried Hiawatha,
Empty-handed, heavy-hearted,
Heard Nokomis moaning, wailing:

5 "Wahonowin! Wahonowin!
Would that I had perished for you,
Would that I were dead as you are!
Wahonowin! Wahanowin!"
And he rushed into the wigwam,
Saw Nokomis rocking, moaning,
Saw his lovely Minnehaha
Lying dead and cold before him.

6 And his bursting heart within him
Uttered such a cry of anguish,
That the very stars in heaven
Shook and trembled with his anguish.
Then he sat down, still and speechless,
On the bed of Minnehaha,

At those willing feet that never
More would lightly run to meet him.

7 With both hands his face he covered,
Seven long days and nights he sat there
As if in a swoon, unconscious
Of the daylight or the darkness.
Then they buried Minnehaha,
Underneath the moaning hemlocks;
Clothed her in her richest garments,
Covered her with snow, like ermine.

8 And at night a fire was lighted,
On her grave four times was kindled,
For her soul upon its journey
To the Islands of the Blessed.
From his sleepless bed uprising,
Hiawatha stood and watched it.
"Farewell!" said he, "Minnehaha!
Farewell, O my Laughing Water!

(From beginning to Fine.)

9 All my heart is buried with you,
All my thoughts go onward with you!
Soon your footsteps I shall follow
To the Islands of the Blessed!"

CHILD AND MOTHER.

Eugene Field.

Arr. from Voigtlaender.

Affettuoso allegretto.

1. O Moth - er - my - Love, if you'll give me your hand, And
2. There'll be no lit - tle tired - out boy to un - dress, No
3. And when I am tired I'll nes - tle my head In the

go where I ask you to wan - der, I will
ques - tions or cares to per - plex you, There'll be
bo - som that's sooth'd me so oft - en, And the

lead you a - way to a beau - ti - ful land,— The
no lit - tle bruis - es or bumps to ca - ress, Nor
wide a - wake stars shall sing in my stead, A

dream - land that's wait - ing out yon - der. We'll
patch - ing of stock - ings to vex you; For I'll
song which our dream - ing shall soft - en. So,

wall in a sweet po - sle - gar - den out there, Where
rock you a - way on a sil - ver - dew stream, And
Moth - er - my - Love, let me take your dear hand, And a -

moon - light and star - light are stream-ing, And the
sing you a - sleep when you're wea - ry, And
way thro' the star - light we'll wan - der,— A -

flowers and the birds are fill - ing the air With the
no one shall know of our beau - ti - ful dream But
way through the mist to the beau - ti - ful land,—The

fra - grance and mu - sic of dream - ing.
you and your own lit - tle dear - ie.
dream - land that's wait - ing out yon - der.

FAITHFUL.

Phoebe Cary.

Arr. from
Wolfgang Amadeus Mozart.

Andante.

1. Faint - er and faint - er may fall on my ear The
2. Whit - er and whit - er may turn with each day The
3. Dark - er and dark - er a - bove thee may spread The

voice that is sweet - er than mu - sic to hear;
locks that so sad - ly are chang-ing to gray;
clouds of a fate that is hope - less and dread;

More and more ea - ger - ly then will I list, That
Dear - er and dear - er shall these seem to me, The
Bright-er and bright-er the sun of my love Will

nev - er a word or an ac - cent be missed.
few - er and whit - er and thin - ner they be.
shine, all the shad - ows and mists to re - move.

Slow - er and slow - er the foot - steps may grow, Whose
Weak - er and weak - er may be the light clasp Of the
En - vy and mal - ice thy life may as - sail,

fall is the pleas - ant - est sound that I know; Whose
hand that I hold so se - cure in my grasp;
Fa - vor and for - tune and friend - ship may fall;

Quick - er and quick - er my glad heart shall learn To
Strong - er and strong - er my own to the last Will
Per - fect and sure, and un - dy - ing shall be The

catch its faint ech - o and bless its re - turn.
cling to it, hold - ing it ten - der - ly fast.
trust of this heart that is cen - tred in thee!

James T. Fields.

Isaac B. Woodbury.

1. We were crowd-ed in the cab-in, Not a
2. So we shud-dered there in sil-ence; For the
3. But his lit-tle daugh-ter whis-pered, As she

soul would dare to sleep; It was mid-night on the
stout-est held his breath, While the hun-gry sea was
took his i - cy hand, "Isn't God up-on the

wa - ters, And a storm was on the deep, 'Tis a
roar - ing, And the break-'ers talked with Death. And as
o - cean, Just the same as on the land ?" Then we

fear - ful thing in win - ter To be shat - tered by the
thus we sat in si - lence, Each bu - sy in his
kissed the lit - tle maid-en, And we spoke in bet - ter

blast, And to　hear the trum - pet　thun - der,　As　he
pray'rs,"We are　lost!" the cap - tain　shout-ed,　As　he
cheer; And we　an - chored safe in　har - bor,　When the

CODA.*

D.C.

"Cut a - way　the　mast!" And a　shout rose wild and
stag - gered down the　stairs.
morn was shin - ing　clear.

joy - ous, As　we　clasped the friend-ly　hand "Ah!

rit.

God is on the　o - cean Just the　same as　on　the　land."

* This spirited coda was, evidently, not written by Mr. Fields, but the editors are not able to say who added it.

Alice Cary. Franz Schubert.

1. O Mem - o - ry, be sweet to me— Take,
2. Take vio - let - bed, and rose - tree red, The
3. Take all of best from east to west, So
4. Ah, Mem - o - ry, be sweet to me! All

take all else at will, So thou but leave me
pur - ple flags by the mill, The mead - ow gay, the
thou but leave me still, The cham - ber, where in the
oth - er foun - tains chill; But leave that song so

safe and sound, With - out a to - ken my
gar - den - ground, But leave, oh leave me,
star - ry light I used to lie a -
weird and wild, Dear as its life to the

heart to wound, The lit - tle house on the hill!
safe and sound, The lit - tle house on the hill!
wake at night And list to the whip - poor - will.
heart of the child, In the lit - tle house on the hill!

Henry Wadsworth Longfellow.   Unknown.

1.   Sol - emn - ly, mourn-ful - ly, Deal - ing its   dole, The
4. No voice in   the cham - bers, No sound in   the hall ! . . .
5. The book is   complet - ed, And closed, like the day; And the
8.   Dark-er   and dark - er   The black shad-ows fall; . . .

Cur - few Bell Is be - gin-ning to toll. 2. Cov-er the em-bers, And
Sleep and ob - liv - i - on Reign o - ver all! D.C.
hand that has writ-ten it Lays it a - way. 6. Dim grow its fan-cies, For-
Sleep and ob - liv - i - on Reign o - ver all!

put out the   light; Toil comes with the morning. And rest with the night.
got-ten they lie; Like coals in the ash-es, They darken and die.

3. Dark grow   the   win - dows, And quenched is the fire;
7. Song sinks in - to si - lence, The sto - ry is told, The

Sound fades in - to si - lence, All foot-steps re - tire.
win - dows are   dark - ened, The hearthstone is cold.

THE BRIDGE.

Henry Wadsworth Longfellow.

M. Lindsay.

Andante con espressione.

1. I stood on the bridge at mid-night, As the
2. How oft-en, O, how oft-en, In the
3. For my heart was hot and rest-less, And my
4. Yet when-ev-er I cross the riv-er On its

clocks were strik-ing the hour, And the
days that had gone by, I had
life was full of care, And the
bridge with wood-en piers, Like the

moon rose o'er the cit-y, Be-
stood on that bridge at mid-night And
bur-den laid up-on me Seemed
o-dor of brine from the o-cean Comes the

hind   the   dark   church tower.   And
gazed on   that   wave   and   sky!   How
great - er   than I   could   bear.   But
thought   of   oth -   er   years.   And for -

like . . those wa - ters rush - ing   A -
oft - en, O, how oft - en,   I had
now It has fall - en from me,   It is
ev - er and for - ev - er,   As

mong the wood - en piers,   A
wished that the ebb - ing tide   Would
bur - ied in the sea;   And
long as the riv - er flows,   As

flood . . of thoughts came o'er me . . That
bear me a - way on its bos - om O'er the
on - ly the sor - row of oth - ers Throws its
long as the heart has pas - sions, As

Verses 1,2,3. *D.C.*

filled my eyes . . . with tears. . . . . . .
o - cean wild . . . and wide! . . . . . .
shad - ow o - ver me . . . .
long as life . . . has

Verses 1,2,3. *D.C.*

Verse 4.

woes; The moon and its bro - ken re -

Verse 4.

flec - tion   And its shad - ows shall   ap -

pear,   As the sym - bol of love   In

heav - en,   And its wav - 'ring im - age here.

THE HERITAGE.

James Russell Lowell. Arr. from the German.

Maestoso.

1. The rich man's son inherits lands, And piles of brick and stone, and gold, And he inherits soft white hands, And tender flesh that fears the cold, And tender flesh that fears the cold; Nor dares to wear a garment old, A heritage, it seems to me, One scarce would wish to hold in fee.

2. What doth the poor man's son inherit? Wishes o'er-joyed with humble things, A rank adjudg'd by toil-won merit, Content that from employment springs, Content that from employment springs, A heart that in his labor sings; A heritage, it seems to me, A king might wish to hold in fee.

3. Both, heirs to some six feet of sod, Are equal in the earth at last; Both, children of the same dear God, Prove title to your heirship vast, Prove title to your heirship vast By record of a well-filled past; A heritage, it seems to me, Well worth a life to hold in fee.

BABY CHARLEY.

Sidney Lanier.   Old College Air.
Allegretto.

1. One arm stretched back-ward round his head, Five
2. Heav'n-lights, I know, are beam-ing through Those
3. O sweet Sleep- An - gel thron - ed now On
4. I vow my heart, when death is nigh, Shall

lit - tle toes from out the bed . . . Just
lu - cent eye - lids, veined with blue, . . . That
the round glo - ry of his brow, . . .
nev - er shiv - er with a sigh . . . For

show - ing like five rose - buds red,— So
shut a - way from mor - tal view Large
Wave thy wing and waft my vow Breathed
act of hand or tongue or eye That

slum - bers Ba - by Char - ley.
eyes of Ba - by Char - ley.
o - ver Ba - by Char - ley.
wronged my Ba - by Char - ley.

WILL AND I.

Paul Hamilton Hayne.

Unknown.

1. We roam the hills to - geth - er,—Will and I, Will and I,
2. Where the tink - ling brook-let pass - es,—Will and I, Will and I,
3. A - mid cool for - est clos - es,—Will and I, Will and I,
4. Ah! thus we roam to - geth - er,—Will and I, Will and I,

In the gold - en sum - mer weath - er,— Will and I: And the
Thro' the heart of dew - y grass - es,— Will and I Have
We have pluck'd the wild - wood ros - es,— Will and I, And have
Thro' the gold - en sum - mer weath - er,— Will and I; While the

glow - ing sun - beams bless us, And the winds of heav'n ca -
heard the mock-bird sing - ing, And the field - lark seen up -
twined, with ten - der du - ty, Sweet wreaths to crown the
glow - ing sun - beams bless us, And the winds of. heav'n ca -

ress us, As we wan - der hand in hand,—Will and I,
spring - ing In his hap - py flight a - far,— Will and I,
beau - ty Of the pur - est brows that shine,—Will and I,
ress us, As we wan - der hand in hand,—Will and I,

Will and I,— Thro' the bliss - ful sum - mer land,— Will and I
Will and I, Like a ti - ny winged star,— Will and I.
Will and I, With a moth - er love di - vine,— Will and I.
Will and I, O'er the bliss - ful sum - mer land,— Will and I.

Eugene Field.   Giovanni Paisiello.

1. Wyn - ken, Blyn - ken, and Nod one night Sailed
2. The old moon laughed and sung a song, As they
3. All night long their nets they threw For the
4. Wyn - ken and Blyn - ken are two lit - tle eyes, And

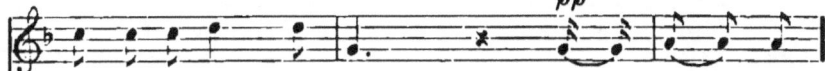

off in a wood - en shoe,— Sailed off on a
rocked in the wood - en shoe; And the wind that
fish in the twink - ling foam, Then down from the
Nod is a lit - tle head, And the wood - en

riv - er of mist - y light In - to a sea of
sped them all night long Ruf - fled the waves of
sky came the wood - en shoe, Bring-ing the fish - er - men
shoe that sailed the skies, A wee one's trun - dle-

dew.   "Where   are   you   go - ing   and
dew;   The   lit - tle   stars   were the
home;   'T was   all   so   pret - ty   a
bed;   So   shut   your   eyes   while

what   do   you   wish?"   The   old   moon asked   the
her - ring - fish   That   lived in   the   beau - ti - ful
sail,   it   seemed   As   if   it   could   not
Moth - er   sings   Of   won - der - ful   sights   that

three.   "We   have   come   to   fish   for   the
sea.   "Now   cast   your   nets . .   wher -
be;   And   some   folks   thought 'twas   a
be,   And   you   shall   see .   the

her - ring fish That live in this beau - ti - ful
ev - er you wish, But nev - er a - feared are
dream they'd dreamed Of sail - ing that beau - ti - ful
beau - ti - ful things As you rock on the mist - y

sea; . . . . . Nets of sil - ver and
we!" . . . . So . . cried the stars to the
sea; . . . . . But . . I shall name you the
sea . . . . . Where the old shoe rocked the

gold have we," Said Wyn - ken, Blyn - ken, and Nod.
fish - er - men three,— Wyn - ken, Blyn - ken, and Nod.
fish - er - men three: Wyn - ken, Blyn - ken, and Nod.
fish - er - men three,— Wyn - ken, Blyn - ken, and Nod.

THE PROPOSAL.

Bayard Taylor.   Arr. from Christoph Willibald Gluck.

1. The vio - let loves a sun - ny bank, The
2. The sun - shine kiss - es mount and vale, The
3. The ori - ole weds his mot - tled mate, The

cow - slip loves the lea; . . . The scar - let creep - er
stars they kiss the sea; . . . The west winds kiss the
lil - y's bride o' the bee; . . . Heav'n's mar - riage - ring is

loves the elm, But I love . . thee. . . .
clov - er bloom, But I kiss . . thee. . . .
round the earth — Shall I wed . . thee? . . .

MAY, THE MAIDEN.

Sidney Lanier.

Joseph Barnby.
(Air: Sweet and Low.)

1. May, the maid - en, Vio - let la - den, Out of the vio - let sea,
2. Day the state - ly, Sunk - en late - ly In - to the vio - let sea,
3. Night the ho - ly, Sail - ing slow - ly O - ver the vio - let sea,

Comes and hov - ers O - ver lov - ers, O - ver thee and me;
Back - ward hov - ers O - ver lov - ers, O - ver me and thee;
Stars un - cov - ers O - ver lov - ers, Stars for me and thee;

O - ver thee, Ma - rie, and me, Out of the vio - let sea, Ma - rie,
O - ver thee, Ma - rie, and me, Out of the vio - let sea, Ma - rie,
Stars for thee, Ma - rie, and me, O - ver the vio - let sea, Ma - rie,

Comes and hovers O - ver lovers, Hovers o - ver thee and me, Ma - rie. . . . .
Backward hovers O - ver lovers, Hovers o - ver thee and me, Ma - rie. . . . .
Stars un - covers O - ver lovers, Stars for lovers, thee and me, Ma - rie. . . . .

IDLE.

Alice Cary.

Friedrich Ludwig Seidel.

Allegretto.

1. I heard the gay spring com - ing, la, la, . . I
2. I heard the ploughman's whis - tle, la, la, . . I
3. I felt the warm, bright weath - er; la, la, . . Saw the
4. The blue bird and her nest - ling, la, la, . . Flew a -

saw the clo - ver bloom - ing, la, la, la, la, la,
saw the rough burr this - tle, la, la, la, la, la,
har - vest, saw them gath - er, la, la, la, la, la,
way;— the leaves fell rust - ling, la, la, la, la, la,

la, . . Red and white a - long the mead - ows;
la, . . In the sharp teeth of the har - row,—
la, . . Corn and mil - let, wheat and ap - ples,—
la, . . The cold rain killed the ros - es, The

IDLE.

p
cres.
Red and white a - long the streams; I heard the blue bird
Saw the sum - mer's yel - low gleams In the wal - nuts, in the
Saw the gray barn's op - 'ning seams, I saw the bare - armed
sun with - drew his beams; . . No crea - ture cared a
dim.
cres.
dim.
sing - ing, I saw the green grass spring - ing, All
fen - nel, In the mul - leins lined with flan - nel, All
shear - ers,— The rud - dy wa - ter bear - ers,— All
bout me, The world could do with - out me, All
rit.
as I lay a dream - ing, A dreaming i - dle dreams.

SHE CAME AND WENT.

James Russell Lowell.

German Air.

Tenderly. Andante.

1. As a twig trem-bles, which a bird Lights on to sing, then
2. As clasps a lake, by gusts un-riven, The blue dome's measure-
3. An an - gel stood and met my gaze, Thro' the low door-way
4. O, when the room grows slow - ly dim, And life's last oil is

leaves un - bent, So is my mem - 'ry thrill'd and stirred; I
less con - tent, So my soul held that mo - ment's heaven; I
of my tent; The tent is struck, the vi - sion stays; I
near - ly spent, One gush of light these eyes will brim, On -

on - ly know she came and went, So is my mem - 'ry
on - ly know she came and went, So my soul held that
on - ly know she came and went, The tent is struck, the
ly to think she came and went, One gush of light these

SHE CAME AND WENT.

thrilled and stirred; I on - ly know she came and went.
mo - ment's heav'n; I on - ly know she came and went.
vi - sion stays; I on - ly know she came and went.
eyes will brim, On - ly to know she came and went.

STARS OF THE SUMMER NIGHT.

Henry Wadsworth Longfellow.

Isaac B. Woodbury.

Slow and gentle.

1. Stars of the sum - mer night! Far in yon az - ure deeps,
2. Moon of the sum - mer night! Far down yon west - ern steeps,
3. Wind of the sum - mer night! Where yon - der wood-bine creeps,
4. Dreams of the sum - mer night! Tell her, her lov - er keeps

Hide, hide your gold - en light! She sleeps! my la - dy sleeps!
Sink, sink in sil - ver light! She sleeps! my la - dy sleeps!
Fold, fold your pin - ions light! She sleeps! my la - dy sleeps!
Watch! while in slum - bers light She sleeps! my la - dy sleeps!

She sleeps! She sleeps! my la - dy sleeps!
She sleeps! She sleeps! my la - dy sleeps!
She sleeps! She sleeps! my la - dy sleeps!
She sleeps! She sleeps! my la - dy sleeps!

NEAR IN THE FOREST.

Bayard Taylor.

Kreipel.

mf   *p*   *mf*

1. Near in the for - est I know a glade, Un - der the
2. There, where the sun - set's lanc - es of gold Pierce, or the
3. Nev - er the breez-es should lisp what we say, Nev - er the

tree - tops a se - cret shade! Vines are the cur - tains,
moon-light is sil - very cold, Would that an an - gel
wa - ters our se - cret be - tray! Si - lence and shad - ow,

blos- soms the floor; Vol - ces of wa - ters sing ev - er -
led thee to me— So, out of lone - li - ness love should
aft - er might reign; But the old life be ours nev - er a -

more. Vines are the cur - tains, blos - soms the floor;
be! Would that an - an - gel led thee to me—
gain! Si - lence and shad - ow, aft - er might reign;

pp   *Rit.*

Vol - ces of wa - ters sing ev - er - more.
So out of lone - li - ness love should be!
But the old life be ours nev - er a - gain!

Phoebe Cary.

Michael Haydn.

1. Watch her kind - ly, kind - ly, stars, Watch her kind - ly,
2. Soothe her sweet - ly, sweet - ly, night, Soothe her sweet - ly,
3. Wake her gent - ly, gent - ly, morn, Wake her gent - ly,

kind - ly, stars; From the sweet, pro - tect - ing skies
sweet - ly, night: On her eyes o'er - wear - ied press The
gent - ly, morn: Let the notes of ear - ly birds

Fol - low her with ten - der eyes, Look so lov - ing -
tir - ed lids with light ca - ress; Let that shadow - y
Seem like love's me - lo - dious words; Ev - 'ry pleas - ant

ly that she Can but think of me.
hand of thine In her dreams seem mine.
sound my dear, When she wakes should hear.

BEN BOLT.

Thomas Dunn English.

Nelson Kneass.

1. Oh! don't you re-mem-ber sweet Al-ice, Ben Bolt.
2. Un - der the hick-o - ry tree, Ben Bolt,
3. And don't you re-mem-ber the school, Ben Bolt,
4. There is change in the things I loved, Ben Bolt,

Sweet Al - ice whose hair was so brown,
Which stood at the foot of the hill,
With the mas - ter so kind and so true,
They have changed from the old to the new,

Who wept with de - light when you gave her a smile.
To - geth - er we've lain in the noon - day shade,
And the shad - ed nook by the run - ning brook,
But I feel in the depths of my spir - it the truth,

And trem-bled with fear at your frown? In the
And list - ened to Ap - ple - ton's mill. The
Where the fair - est wild flow-ers grew? Grass
There nev - er was change in you.

old   church - yard,   in   the   val - ley,   Ben   Bolt,
mill - wheel has fal - len to piec - es,   Ben   Bolt,
grows   on   the   mas - ter's   grave,   Ben   Bolt,
Twelve - months   twen - ty   have   passed,   Ben   Bolt,

In   a   cor - ner   ob - scure   and   a - lone;
The   raf - ters   have tum - bled   in,
The   spring of   the   brook   is   dry,
Since   first   we   were friends — yet   I   hail

They have fit - ted   a   slab   of   the gran - ite so   gray, And sweet
And   a   qui-et   that crawls round the   walls as you   gaze, Has
And of   all   the   boys   who   were school - mates then, There are
Thy   presence a   bless - ing,   thy friendship   a   truth, Ben

Al - ice   lies   un - der   the   stone,   - der   the stone.
fol - lowed   the   old - en   din,   - en   din.
on - ly   you   and   I,   and   I.
Bolt of   the   salt   sea   gale,   sea   gale.

THE KATYDID.

Oliver Wendell Holmes.

German Air.

1. O tell me where did Ka - ty live, And
2. Dear me! I'll tell you all a - bout My
3. Ah no! the liv - ing oak shall crash, That

what did Ka - ty do? . . . . . And was she ve - ry
fuss with lit - tle Jane, ... And Ann, with whom I
stood for a - ges still, ... The rock shall rend its

fair and young, And yet so wick - ed, too? Did
used to walk So oft - en down the lane, And
mos - sy base And thun - der down the hill, Be -

Ka - ty love a - naugh-ty man, Or kiss more cheeks than
all that tore their locks of black, Or wet their eyes of
fore the lit - tle Ka - ty - did Shall add one word, to

one? I war - rant Ka - ty did no more
blue,— I'ray tell me, sweet - est Ka - ty - did,
tell The mys - tic sto - ry of the maid

Than many a Kate has done, done.
What did poor Ka - ty do, do?
Whose name she knows so well, well.

A DREAM OF SUMMER.

John Greenleaf Whittier.　　　　　　　　　　　　German Air.

1. Bland as the morn-ing breath of June The southwest breez-es play; And, thro' its haze, the win-ter noon Seems warm as sum-mer's day. The snow-plumed An-gel of the North Has dropp'd his i-cy spear; A-gain the moss-y

2. The fox his hill-side cell forsakes, The muskrat leaves his nook, The blue-bird in the mead-ow brakes Is sing-ing with the brook. "Bear up, O Moth-er Na-ture!" cry Bird, breeze, and streamlet free; "Our win-ter voic-es

3. So, in those win-ters of the soul, By bit-ter blasts and drear, O'er-swept from Mem-ory's fro-zen pole, Will sun-ny days ap-pear. Re-viv-ing Hope and Faith, they show The soul its liv-ing pow'rs, And how be-neath the

4. The Night is moth-er of the Day, The Win-ter of the Spring, And ev-er up-on old De-cay The green-est moss-es cling. Be-hind the cloud the star-light lurks, Thro' show'rs the sunbeams fall; For God, who lov-eth

earth looks forth, A - gain the streams gush clear, streams gush clear.
proph - e - sy Of sum- mer days to thee, days to thee!"
win - ter's snow Lie germs of sum - mer flow'rs, sum - mer flow'rs!
all His works, Has left His Hope with all, Hope with all!

THINE EYES STILL SHINED.

Ralph Waldo Emerson.　　　　　Konradin Kreutzer.

1. Thine eyes still shined for me, tho' far I
2. When the red - bird spread his sa - ble wing, And

roved the land or sea: As I be - hold yon
showed his side of flame; When the rose - bud ri - pened

even - ing star, Which yet be - holds not me. This
to the rose, In both I read thy name. Thine

morn I climbed the mist - y hill And roam'd the pas - tures through; How
eyes still shined for me, tho' far I roved the land or sea: As

danced thy form be - fore my path, A - midst the deep - eyed dew!
I be - hold yon even-ing star, Which yet be - holds not me.

Phoebe Cary.

W. G. Becker.

1. Of what are you think - ing, my pret - ty maid, With your feet in the sum - mer clo - ver? Ah! you need not hang your mod - est head; I know 'tis a - bout your lov - er.

2. I know by the blush - es up - on your cheek, Tho' you strive to hide the tok - en; And I know be - cause you will not speak The thought that is un - spok - en.

3. You are count - ing the pet - als, one by one, Of your dain - ty dew - y po - sies, To find from their num - ber, when 'tis done, The se - cret it dis - clos - es.

4. Be - ware, be - ware, what you say and do, Fair maid, with your feet in the clo - ver; For the poor - est man that comes to woo, May be the rich - est lov - er.

THE SUMMERS COME AND GO.

Bayard Taylor.

Johann A. P. Schulz.

Andante. *mf*

1. Now the days are brief and drear: Na - ked
2. Leave the clash - ing cym - bals mute! Pipe no
3. Where is Youth? He strayed a - way Thro' the
4. Yet a few more years to run, Wheel - ing

lies the new - born Year, In his crad - le of the
more the hap - py flute! Sing no more that dan - cing
mead - ow flow'rs of May; Where is Love? The leaves that
round in gloom and sun: Oth - er rap - tures, oth - er

snow; And the winds un - bri - dled blow, And the
rhyme Of the ro - se's har - vest time; Sing a
fell From his tryst - ing - bow'r, can tell. Wis - dom
woes,— Toil al - ter - nate with Re - pose: Then to

skies hang dark and low,— For the Sum - mers come and go.
re - quiem, sad and low, For the Sum - mers come and go.
stays, se - date and slow: And the Sum - mers come and go.
sleep where dai - sies grow, While the Sum - mers come and go.

NOVEMBER.

Judson Hutchinson.
(Air: The Old Granite State.)

Alice Cary.

1. The leaves are fad - ing and fall - ing, The
2. And when the win - ter is o - ver, The
3. The leaves to - day are whirl - ing The

winds are rough and wild, The birds have ceased their
boughs will get new leaves, The quail come back to the
brooks are dry and dumb, But let me tell you, my

pp

call - ing,   But let   me tell you, my child,   Though
clo - ver,   The swal - low come back to   the eaves.   The
dar - ling,   The spring will be   sure   to   come.   So,

day   by   day, as it   clos - es,   Doth dark-er   and cold - er
rob - in   will wear on his   bo - som   A   vest that is   bright and
when   some dear   joy   los - es   Its   beau-te - ous sum - mer

grow,   The   roots of the   bright   red   ros - es   Will
new,   And the love - li - est   way - side blos - som   Will
glow,   Think   how   the roots of the   ros - es   Are

dim.

Henry Wadsworth Longfellow.

John Hullah.

1. The day is end - ing, The night is de - scend - ing; The
2. The snow re - com - men - ces; The bur - ied fen - ces
3. The bell is peal - ing, And ev - 'ry feel - ing With -

marsh is fro - zen, The riv - er is dead. Through
Mark no long - er The road o'er the plain; While
in me re - sponds To the dis - mal knell;

clouds like ash - es The red sun flash - es On
through the mead - ows, Like fear - ful shad - ows,
Shad - ows are trail - ing, My heart is be - wail - ing And

vil - lage win - dows That glim - mer red.
Slow - ly pass - es A fun - 'ral train.
toll - ing with - in Like a fun - 'ral bell.

THE HUMBLE-BEE.

Ralph Waldo Emerson.

German Air

1. Bur - ly, doz - ing hum - ble - bee, Where thou art is
2. When the south wind, in May days, With a net of
3. Hot mid - sum - mer's pet - ted crone, Sweet to me thy
4. Wis - er far than hu - man seer, Yel - low - breeched phi -

clime for me. Let them sail for Por - to Rique,
shin - ing haze Sil - vers the hor - i - zon wall,
drow - sy tone Tells of count - less sun - ny hours,
los - o - pher! See - ing on - ly what is fair,

Far - off heats through seas to seek; I will fol - low
And with soft - ness touch - es all, Thou, in sun - ny
Long days, sol - id banks of flowers; Aught un - sav - 'ry
Thou dost mock at fate and care; When the fierce north -

thee a - lone, Thou an - i - mat - ed tor - rid zone!
sol - i - tudes, Ro - ver of the un - der - woods,
or un - clean Hath my in - sect nev - er seen;
west - ern blast Cools sea and land so far and fast,

Let me chase thy wav-ing lines, Sing-ing o-ver shrubs and vines.
The green si-lence dost dis-place With thy mel-low breezy bass.
Clov-er, catch-fly, ad-der's tongue, Bri-er ro-ses, dwelt a-mong.
Thou al-read-y slum-b'rest deep; Woe and want thou canst out-sleep.

WOODNOTES.

Ralph Waldo Emerson.   Wenzel Müller.

1. He loved the wild, a for-est seer, A min-strel
2. It seemed that Na-ture could not raise A plant in
3. He saw the part-ridge drum in the woods; He heard the
4. What oth-ers did at dis-tance hear, And guessed with-

of the nat-ural year, A lov-er true, who knew by
an-y se-cret place, But he would come the ver-y
wood-cock's ev'n-ing hymn; He found the tawn-y thrush-es'
in the thick-et's gloom, Was shown to this phil-os-o-

heart Each joy the moun-tain dales im-part.
hour It o-pened in its vir-gin bower.
broods; And the shy hawk did wait for him.
pher, And at his bid-ding seemed to come.

THE FOUNTAIN.

James Russell Lowell.

German Air.
(Air: Buy a Broom.)

1. In - to the sun - shine, Full of the light,
2. In - to the star - light Rush - ing in spray,
3. Glad of all weath-ers, Still seem-ing best,
4. Cease - less as - pir - ing, Cease-less con - tent.

Leap - ing and flash-ing From morn till night!
Hap - py at mid - night, Hap-py by day!
Up - ward or down-ward, Mo - tion thy rest; —
Dark - ness or sun - shine Thy el - e - ment; —

In - to the moon-light, Whit - er than snow,
Ev - er in mo - tion, Blithe - some and cheer-y,
Full of a na - ture Noth - ing can tame,
Glo - ri - ous foun - tain! Let my heart be

Wav - ing so flower-like When the winds blow!
Still climb - ing heaven-ward, Nev - er a - weary; —
Changed ev - 'ry mo - ment, Ev - er the same; —
Fresh, changeful, con - stant, Up - ward, like thee!

John Greenleaf Whittier.　　　　　　　　　　　　　German Air.

1. The harp at Na-ture's ad - vent strung Has nev - er ceased to
2. The green earth sends her in - cense up From many a moun - tain
3. The mists a - bove the morn-ing rills Rise white as wings of
4. The winds with hymns of praise are loud, Or low with sobs of
5. The blue sky is the tem - ple's arch, Its tran - sept earth and

play; The song the stars of morn - ing sung Has
shrine; From fold - ed leaf and dew - y cup She
prayer; The al - tar-cur - tains of the hills Are
pain,— The thun - der or - gan of the cloud, The
air, The mu - sic of its star - ry march The

nev - er died a - way, Has nev - er died a - way.
pours her sa - cred wine, She pours her sa - cred wine.
sun - set's pur - ple air, Are sun - set's pur - ple air.
drop-ping tears of rain, The drop - ping tears of rain.
cho - rus of a prayer, The cho - rus of a prayer

THE LIGHT THAT IS FELT.

John Greenleaf Whittier.　　　　　　　Albert Gotlieb Methfessel.

Tenderly.

1. A ten-der child of summers three, Seeking her lit-tle
2. We old-er chil-dren grope our way From dark be-hind to
3. Reach downward to the sun-less days Wherein our guides are

bed at night, Paused on the dark stair tim-id-ly, "O
dark be-fore; And on-ly when our hands we lay, Dear
blind as we, And faith is small and hope de-lays; Take

moth-er! take my hand" said she, "And then the dark will
Lord, in Thine, the night is day, And there is dark-ness
Thou the hand of prayer we raise, And let us feel the

all   be light, And   then the   dark will all   be   light."
nev - er- more, And   there is   dark-ness nev - er - more.
light   of Thee, And   let   us   feel the   light   of   Thee.

GONE.

John Greenleaf Whittier.   Theodore Stein.

Andante.

1. An - oth - er hand is beck'ning us, An - oth - er call   is   given;
2. As   pure and sweet, her fair brow seem'd E - ter - nal as   the sky;
3. And half we deem'd she needed not The changing of   her sphere,
4. There seems a shad -ow on the day, Her smile no long - er cheers;
5. A - lone un - to   our Father's will One thought hath recon - ciled;

And   glows once more with An - gel-steps The path which reaches Heaven.
And   like   the brook's low song, her voice,—A sound which could not die.
To   give   to heav'n a   Shin- ing One, Who walked an An - gel here.
A   dim - ness on   the stars of night, Like eyes that look thro' tears.
That He   whose love ex - ceed- eth ours Hath ta - ken home His child.

DON'T BE SORROWFUL, DARLING.

Alice Cary.   J. P. Webster.

1. Ah, don't be sor-row-ful, dar-ling, And
2. We are old folks now, my dar-ling, . Our
3. And God is God, my dar-ling, Of

don't be sor-row-ful, pray, ... For,
heads they are grow-ing gray, ... But
night as well as of day, ... But we

tak-ing the year to-geth-er, my dear, There
tak-ing the year all a-round, my dear, You will
feel and know that we can go, Wher -

is n't   more night than   day! . . .   'Tis   rain - y
al -   ways   find   the   May! . . .   We have had our
ev - er   He   leads the   way. . . .   Aye,   God of the

weath-er, my dar - ling, . .   Time's waves, they heav - i - ly
May,   my   dar - ling, . .   And our ros - es,   long   a -
night, my   dar - ling— . .   Of the night   of   death,   so

run, ...   But   tak - ing the   year   to -
go, ...   And the time of the   year   is
grim! . . . . .   The   gate that leads out   of

geth-er, my dear, There isn't more cloud than sun! . .
com-ing, my dear, For the si-lent night and the snow!. .
life, good wife, Is the gate that leads to Him. . .

CHORUS.

Then, don't be sor-row-ful, dar-ling. . . Don't be

sor-row-ful, pray; . . . For, tak-ing the year to-

geth-er, my dear, There isn't more night than day. . .

Bayard Taylor.

English Air.

1. Learn to live, and live to learn, Ig - no - rance like a fire doth burn, Lit - tle tasks make large re-turn; Learn to live, and live to learn.

2. In thy la - bors pa - tient be, Af - ter - ward, re - leased and free, Na - ture will be bright to thee; In thy la - bors pa - tient be.

3. Toil, when will - ing, grow - eth less; "Al - ways play" may seem to bless, Yet the end is wea - ri - ness; Toil, when will-ing, grow-eth less.

4. Live to learn, and learn to live, On - ly this con - tent can give; Reck - less joys are fu - gi - tive! — Live to learn, and learn to live.

THE POET.

Ralph Waldo Emerson.

Friedrich Wilhelm Kücken.

1. Let me go wher-e'er I will, where'er I will, . . I
2. Let me go wher-e'er I will, where'er I will, . . I
3. Let me go wher-e'er I will, where'er I will, . . I

hear a sky - born mu - sic still; It sounds from all things
hear a sky - born mu - sic still; Not on - ly in the
hear a sky - born mu - sic still; Not in the stars a -

old, It sounds from all things young, From all that's fair or foul peals out a
rose, Not on - ly in the bird, Nor on-ly in the song of wo-man
lone, Nor cups of bud-ding flow'rs, The red-breast's tone, the bow that smiles in

song! From all that's fair, from all that's foul, Peals
heard. Not on - ly in the rose, or bird, Nor
showers. Not stars a - lone, or bud -ding flowers, The

out a cheer - ful, cheer - ful song, And in the dark - est,
in the song of wo - man heard, But in the dark - est,
bird, or bow that smiles in showers, But in the dark - est,

mean - est things, There al - way, al-way something sings.

BABY'S RING.

Phoebe Cary.

English Air.

1. Moth-er's quite dis-tract-ed, Sis-ter's in des-pair,
2. Sure-ly nev-er such a babe Made a moth-er glad;
3. When she comes to wo-man-hood, If she keeps so fair,

All the household is a-stir Search-ing ev-'ry-where.
Nev-er such a dain-ty hand An-y ba-by had!
She will sure-ly wear the ring Maid-ens love to wear:

Ev-'ry nook must be ex-plored, Ev-'ry cor-ner scanned—
Small-est ring was ev-er made Off her fin-ger slips;
And lest she should lose it then, She'll be wise and deep,

Ba - by's lost the ti - ny ring From her lit - tle hand.
She should have a fair - y's ring For such ro - sy tips.
She will give to somebod - y Ring and hand to keep.

ALIKE ARE LIFE AND DEATH.

Henry Wadsworth Longfellow.   Christian Heinrich Rinck.

Andante.

1. A - like are life and death, When life in death sur - vives,
2. Were a star quenched on high, For a - ges would its light,
3. So when a great man dies, For years be - yond our ken,

And the un - in - ter - rupt - ed breath In - spires a thousand lives.
Still trav - 'ling downward from the sky, Shine on our mor - tal sight.
The light he leaves be - hind him lies Up - on the paths of men.

THE OLD YEAR AND THE NEW.

John Godfrey Saxe.

J. M. Sayles.
(Air: Beautiful Star.)

1. Good - by, Old Year! I can but say,
2. Good - by, Old Year! O lit - tle in - deed
3. Good - by, Old Year! with words of grace

Sad - ly I see thee pass - ing a - way;
Thy friend-ly voice we were wont to heed;
Leave us with him who takes thy place; And

Pass - ing a - way with the hopes and fears, The
Tell - ing us, warn-ing us ev - 'ry day!
say, Old Year, un - to the new,

dim.

bliss and pain, the smiles and tears, That
Tran - sient mor - tals! work and pray;
Kind - ly, care-ful - ly, car - ry them through, For

dim.

come to us in all the years.
You, like me are pass - ing a - way.
much, I ween, they have yet to do.

Chorus.

mp

cres.

Good-by, Old Year, . . . I can but say, . . .

p

Good-by, Old Year, I can but say.

f *dim.*

Sad - ly I see thee pass - ing, pass-ing a - way.

f *dim.*

TO MOTHER FAIRIE.

Alice Cary.

Unknown.
(Air: What's a' the steer, Kimmer?)

Recitativo.

1.　　Good old moth - er Fair - ie,　　Sit - ting by your
2. To　chase a - way　the shad - ows　That make her moan and

fire,　　　Have　you　an - y　lit - tle　folk
weep,　　　To　sing　her　lov - ing　lul - la - bies,　And

You would like　to hire?　I　want no chub - by drudg - es　To
kiss her　eyes a - sleep;　And when in dreams she reach - es　For

milk, and churn, and spin,   Nor old and wrink-led Brown-ies, With
pleas - ures dead and gone,   To hold her was - ted fin - gers, And

gris - ly beards, and thin: But pa - tient lit - tle
make the rings stay on.   They must be ver - y

peo - ple.   With hands of bus - y care,   And
cun - ning   To make the fu - ture shine   Like

TO MOTHER FAIRIE.

gen - tle speech, and lov - ing hearts; Say, have you such to spare?
leaves, and flow'rs, and strawber-ries, A grow - ing on one vine;

I know a poor, pale bod - y, Who can - not sleep at night,
So good old moth-er Fai - rie, Since now my need you know,

And I want the lit - tle peo-ple To keep her cham - ber bright.
Tell me, have you a - ny folk, Who are wise e - nough to go?

John Greenleaf Whittier.   Joseph B. Sharland.

Andante. (*Not slow.*)

1. Re - vive a - gain, thou sum - mer rain, The bro - ken turf up -
2. With calm and beau - ty sym - bo - lize The peace which fol - lows
2. For safe with right and truth he is, As God lives he must

on his bed! Breathe, sum - mer wind, thy ten - d'rest strain Of
long an - noy, And lend our earth - bent, mourn - ing eyes Some
live al - way; There is no end for souls like his, No

low, sweet mu - sic o - ver - head, sweet mu - sic o - ver - head!
hint of his di - vin - er joy, of his di - vin - er joy.
night for chil - dren of the day, for chil - dren of the day!

THE OPEN WINDOW.

Henry Wadsworth Longfellow.   Alfred Scott Gatty.

Andante con molto espressione.

1. The old house by the lin - dens Stood si - lent in the shade, And on the grav - elled
2. The large New - found-land house-dog Was stand-ing by the door; He looked for his lit - tle
3. The birds sang in the branch-es With sweet, fa - mil - lar tone; But the vol - ces of the

path - way The light and shad - ow played. I
play - mates, Who would re - turn no more. They
chil - dren Will be heard in dreams a - lone! And the

piu lento.

saw the nur - s'ry win-dows Wide o - pen to the air, But the
walked not un - der the lin - dens, They played not in the hall; But
boy that walked be - side me, He could not un - der - stand Why

piu lento.

fa - ces of the chil - dren, They were no long - er there.
shad - ow, and si - lence, and sad - ness Were hang-ing o - ver all.
clos - er in mine, ah! clos - er, I press'd his warm, soft hand!

MY PSALM.

John Greenleaf Whittier.

Wolfgang Amadeus Mozart.

Allegretto.

1. I mourn no more my van-ished years: Be-neath a ten-der
2. The airs of spring may nev-er play A-mong the ripen-ing
3. All as God wills, who wise-ly heeds To give or to with-
4. That care and tri-al seem at last, Thro' mem-'ry's sun-set

rain, An A-pril rain of smiles and tears, My
corn, Nor fresh-ness of the flowers of May Blow
hold, And know-eth more of all my needs Than
air, Like moun-tain-ran-ges o-ver-past, In

heart is young a-gain. The west-winds blow, and,
through the au-tumn morn; Yet shall the blue-eyed
all my prayers have told! E-nough that bless-ings
pur-ple dis-tance fair:— And so the shad-ows

sing-ing low, I hear the glad streams run; The
gen-tian look Thro' fring-ed lids to heaven, And
un-de-served Have marked my err-ing track;— That
fall a-part, And so the west-winds play; And

win - dows of my soul I throw Wide o - pen to the sun.
the pale as - ter in the brook Shall see its im - age given.
whereso - e'er my feet have swerv'd, His chastening turned me back; —
all the win - dows of my heart I o - pen to the day.

NEARER HOME.
A CHANT.

Phoebe Cary.
Solemnly.

1. One sweetly sol - emn thought Comes
2. Nearer my Fa - ther's house, Where the
3. Nearer the bound of life, Where we
4. But lying darkly be - tween, Wind-ing

to me o'er and o'er; I am nearer home to -
ma - ny man - sions be; Nearer the great white
lay our bur - dens down, Nearer leaving the
down through the night, Is the silent, unknown

day Than I ever have been be - fore.
throne, Nearer the crystal sea;
cross, Nearer gaining the crown!
stream, That leads at last to the light.

THE RAINY DAY.

Henry Wadsworth Longfellow.　　　　　William Richardson Dempster.

1. The day is cold, and dark, and drea - ry; It
2. My life is cold, and dark, and drea - ry; It
3. Be still, sad heart! and cease re - pin - ing; Be -

rains, and the wind is nev - er wea-ry; The vine still
rains, and the wind is nev - er wea-ry; My thoughts still
hind the clouds is the sun still shin-ing; Thy fate is the

clings to the moul - d'ring wall, But at ev - 'ry
cling to the moul - d'ring Past, But the hopes of
com - mon fate of all, In - to each

gust   the   dead   leaves   fall,   And the   day   is   dark   and
youth   fall   thick   in the   blast,   And the   days   are   dark   and
life   some   rain   must   fall,   Some   days   must be   dark   and

drea - ry, ...   And the   day   is   dark   and
drea - ry, ...   And the   days   are   dark   and
drea - ry, ...   Some   days   must be   dark   and

drea - ry, ...   And the   day   is   dark   and   drea - ry.
drea - ry, ...   And the   days   are   dark   and   drea - ry.
drea - ry, ...   Some   days   must be   dark   and   drea - ry.

PLEASURE-PAIN.

William Dean Howells.

Halfdan Kjerulf.

1. Full of beau - ti - ful
2. But all thro' the glow - ing
3. In youth there comes a

blos - soms Stood the tree in ear - ly May: Came a
sum - mer The blossom - less tree throve fair, And the
west - wind Blowing our blossoms a - way,— A

chil - ly gale from the sun - set, And blew . . . the
fruit waxed ripe and mel - low, With sun - - ny
chil - ly breath of Au - tumn Out of the

blossoms a - way; And scat-tered them through the gar - den,
rain and air; And when the dim Oc - to - ber With
lips of May. We bear the ripe fruit aft - er,— Ah,

Tossed them in - to the mere: . . The sad tree moaned and
gold - en death was crowned, Un - der its heav - y,
me! for the tho't of pain!— We know the sweet - ness,

shuddered, "A - las! . . . A - las! the Fall is
groan - ing branch - es The tree stooped to the
and the beau - ty, And heart - bloom nev - er a -

here."
ground.
gain.

I KNOW NOT WHAT THE FUTURE HATH.

John Greenleaf Whittier.   W. Irmer.

1. I   know not what the   fu - ture hath Of   mar - vel or sur - prise,
2. And so   be - side the   Si - lent Sea I   wait the muf-fled   oar;
3. I   know not where His   is - lands lift Their fronded palms in   air;
4. And Thou, O   Lord! by   Whom are seen Thy   crea - tures as   they be,

As - sured a - lone that life   and death His mer - cy un - der - lies.
No harm from Him can   come to me On   o - cean or on   shore.
I   on - ly know I   can - not drift Be - yond His love and   care.
For - give me if   too   close I   lean My   hu - man heart on   Thee.

Henry Wadsworth Longfellow.

A. ten Cate.

1. Stay, stay at home, my heart, and rest; Homekeeping hearts
2. Weary and home - sick and dis - tressed, They wan - der east,
3. Then stay at home, my heart, and rest; The bird is saf -

are hap - pi - est, For those that wan - der they
they wan - der west, And are baf - fled and beat - en and
est in the nest; O'er all that flut - ter their

know not where, Are full of trouble and full of care; To
blown a - bout By the winds of the wil - der - ness of doubt; To
wings and fly A hawk is hov - 'ring in the sky; To

stay at home is best, To stay at home is best.

THE FATHERLAND.

James Russell Lowell.

C. G. Bellmann.

1.   Where Is the true man's fa - ther - land? Is it
2. Wher - e'er   a   hu - man   heart doth wear   Joy's
3. Wher - e'er   a   sin - gle   slave doth pine,   Where

where he by chance was born? Doth not   the yearn - ing spir - it
wreath or   sor - row's gyves, Where'er   a   hu - man spir - it
one   man may help an - other,—Thank God   for such   a   birth - right,

scorn   In such   scant bor - ders to   be   spanned?
strives   Af - ter a   life more true and fair,
broth - er, That spot of   earth is thine and mine!

CHORUS.

O yes, his   fa - ther - land must be   As   the blue
There is the   true man's birth - place grand, His is   a
There is the   true man's birth - place grand, His is   a

heav - en, wide and free! Yes, his   fa - ther - land must
world - wide fa - ther - land! There is the true man's birthplace
world - wide fa - ther - land! There is the true man's birthplace

be   As   the blue heav - en, wide and free!
grand, His is   a   world - wide fa - ther - land!
grand, His is   a   world - wide fa - ther - land!

WHAT THE CHIMNEY SANG.

Francis Bret Harte.   Edwin G. Hopkins.

1. O - ver the chim - ney the night-wind sang, And chant - ed a
2. O - ver the chim - ney the night-wind sang, And chant - ed a
3. O - ver the chim - ney the night-wind sang, And chant - ed a
4. O - ver the chim - ney the night-wind sang, And chant - ed a

mel - o - dy   no   one knew; And the Wo - man stopped, as her
mel - o - dy   no   one knew; And the Chil - dren said, as they
mel - o - dy   no   one knew; And the Man, as he sat on his
mel - o - dy   no   one knew; But the Po - et list - ened and

babe   she   toss'd,   And   thought of the one   she had
clos - er   drew,   "'T is some witch   that is cleav - ing the
hearth be - low,   Said   to him-self, "It   will
smil'd, for   he   Was   Man   and   Wo - man, and

long   since lost,   And   said,   as   her   tear - drops
black night thro' —   'T is a fai - ry   trum - pet that
sure - ly   snow,   And   fu - el is   dear   and
Child, all   three,   And   said, "It is   God's   own

back she forced. "I hate the wind in the chim - ney."
just then blew, And we fear the wind in the chim - ney."
wa - ges low, And I'll stop the leak in the chim - ney."
har - mo - ny, This wind we hear in the chim - ney."

LORD OF ALL BEING.

Oliver Wendell Holmes.   Francis Linley.

1. Lord of all be - ing! throned a - far, Thy glo - ry
2. Sun of our life, thy quick - 'ning ray Sheds on our
3. Lord of all life, be - low, a - bove, Whose light is
4. Grant us thy truth to make us free, And kind - ling

flames in sun and star; Cen - tre and soul of
path the glow of day; Star of our hope, thy
truth, whose warmth is love, Be - fore thy ev - er -
hearts that burn for thee, Till all thy liv - ing

ev - 'ry sphere, Yet to each lov - ing heart how near!
soft - en'd light Cheers the long watch - es of the night.
blaz - ing throne We ask no lus - tre of our own.
al - tars claim One ho - ly light, one heav'n - ly flame!

Harriet Beecher Stowe.
William H. Hutchinson.

1. Cease, cease to think, but be con-tent to be; Swing safe at an-
2. Call not such hours an i - dle waste of time,—Land that lies fal-

chor in fair Nature's bay, Rea - son no more, but o'er thy qui - et
low gains a quiet power; It treas-ures, from the brood-ing of God's

soul Let God's sweet teach-ings rip - ple their soft way.   Soar with the
wings, Strength to un - fold the fu - ture tree and flower. And when the

birds, and flut-ter with the leaf;   Dance with the seed - ed
sum - mer's glo-rious show is past, Its mir - a - cles no

grass in fring-y play; Sail with the cloud, wave with the
long-er charm thy sight, The treas-ured rich-es of those

dream-ing pine, And float with Na-ture all the live-long day.
thought-ful hours Shall make thy win-try mus-ings warm and bright.

THE REAPER AND THE FLOWERS.

Henry Wadsworth Longfellow.   L. O. Emerson.

1. There is a Reaper, whose name is Death, And, with his sick-le keen,
2. "Shall I have naught that is fair?" saith he; "Have naught but the beard-ed grain?
3. He gazed at the flowers with tearful eyes, He kissed their droop-ing leaves;
4. "My Lord has need of these flow'rets gay," The Reaper said, and smiled;
5. "They shall all bloom in fields of light, Transplanted by my care,
6. And the mother gave, in tears and pain, The flowers she most did love;
7. O, not in cruelty, not in wrath, The Reaper came that day;

He reaps the bearded grain at a breath, And the flow'rs that grow be-tween.
Tho' the breath of these flowers is sweet to me, I will give them back a-gain."
It was for the Lord of Paradise He bound them in his sheaves.
"Dear tokens of the earth are they, Where he was once a child."
And saints, upon their garments white, These sa-cred blos-soms wear."
She knew she should find them all again In the fields of light a-bove.
'Twas an angel visited the green earth, And took the flow'rs a-way.

Thomas Bailey Aldrich.

Wolfgang Amadeus Mozart.

Allegretto.

1. Just   as   the   moon   was   fa - ding   a -
2. "Quite   like   a   stock-ing,"   he   laughed,   "hung

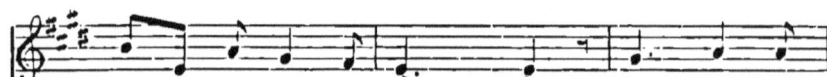

mid   her   mis - ty   rings, . . .   And   ev - 'ry
up   there on   the   tree! . . .   I   didn't sup -

stock-ing   was   stuffed   with   child - hood's pre - cious
pose   the   birds   ex - pect - ed   a   pres - ent from

things, . . Old Kriss Krin-gle looked round and saw up-
me!" . . Then old Kriss Krin-gle, who loves a joke as

on the elm-tree bough, High hung an
well as the best, Dropped a handful of

o - ri - ole's nest, . . . lone-ly and emp - ty now.
snow - flakes in - to the o - ri - ole's emp - ty nest.

LONG TIME AGO.

George Pope Morris.

Charles Edward Horn.

1. Near the lake where drooped the wil-low, Long time a-go!
2. Rock, and tree, and flow-ing wa-ter, Long time a-go!
3. Min-gled were our hearts for-ev-er, Long time a-go!

Where the rock threw back the bil-low, Bright-er than snow!
Bird, and bee, and blos-som taught her Love's spell to know.
Can I now for-get her? nev-er! No, lost one, no!

Dwelt a maid be-loved and cher-ished By high and low;
While to my fond words she list-ened, Mur-mur-ing low,
To her grave these tears are giv-en, Ev-er to flow!

But with Au-tumn's leaf she per-ished, Long time a-go!
Ten-der-ly her dove-eyes glist-ened, Long time a-go!
She's the star I missed from heaven, Long time a-go!

Arr. from E. E. Whittemore.

Moderato

1. Kind words can nev - er die, nev-er die, Cher - ished and blest;
2. Sweet tho'ts can nev - er die, nev-er die, Tho' like the flowers,
3. Child - hood can nev - er die, nev-er die, Wrecks of the past

cres. *f*

God knows how deep they lie, . . Stored in the breast.
Their bright-est hues may fly, . . In win - try hours:
Float o'er the mem - o - ry, . . Bright to the last,

cres. *f*

God knows how deep they lie,
The bright-est hues may fly,
Float o'er the mem-o - ry,

Like childhood's simple rhymes, Said
But when the gentle dew Gives
Ma - ny a hap-py thing, Ma -

Like child-hood's sim - ple rhymes Said o'er a thou - sand
But when the gen - tle dew Gives them their charms a -
Ma - ny a hap - py thing, Ma - ny a bloom - ing

pp *rit.*

o'er a thousand times, Aye, in all years and climes, Dis - tant and near.
them their charms anew, with many an add - ed hue, They bloom a - gain.
ny a blooming spring, Float o'er life's ceaseless wing, Far, far a - way.

pp

times,
new,
spring,

WALDEINSAMKEIT.

Ralph Waldo Emerson.

Felix Mendelssohn-Bartholdy.

1. I do not count the hours I spend In wan-d'ring by the sea;
2. In plains that room for shad-ows make Of skirt-ing hills to lie,
3. See thou bring not to fields or stone The fan - cies found in books;

The for - est is my loy - al friend, Like God it us - eth me.
Bound in by streams which give and take Their col - ors from the sky;
Leave au - thors' eyes, and fetch your own, To brave the landscape's looks;

A - loft, in se - cret veins of air, Blows the sweet breath of song, O
Or on the mountain-crest sub-lime, Or down the o - pen glade, O
Ob - liv - ion here thy wis - dom is, Thy thrift, the sleep of cares; For

few to scale these up - lands dare,Tho' they to all be - long, O
what have I to do with time? For this the day was made, O
a proud i - dle - ness like this Crowns all thy mean af - fairs, For

cres. *dim.* *pp* to all

few to scale these up-lands dare, Tho' they to all be - long.
what have I to do with time? For this the day was made.
a proud i - dle - ness like this Crowns all thy mean af - fairs.

cres. *dim.* *pp*

SOFTLY NOW THE LIGHT OF DAY.

George Washington Doane.　　　　Friedrich Wilhelm Kücken.

1. Soft - ly now the light of day Fades up - on our sight a -
2. Soon for us the light of day Shall for - ev - er pass a -

way;　Free from care, from labor free　Lord, we
way;　Then from sin and labor free,　Take us,

would com - mune with Thee, Lord, we would com - mune with Thee.
Lord, to dwell with Thee, Take us, Lord, to dwell with Thee.

NEARER, MY GOD, TO THEE.

Sarah Flower Adams.   Lowell Mason.

1. Near - er, my God, to Thee, Near - er to Thee:
2. Tho' like a wan - der - er, Day - light all gone,
3. There let the way ap - pear Steps up to heav'n;
4. Then, with my wak - ing tho'ts Bright with Thy praise,

E'en though it be a cross That rais - eth me;
Dark - ness be o - ver me, My rest a stone;
All that Thou send - est me, In mer - cy giv'n;
Out of my ston - y griefs, Beth - el I'll raise;

Still all my song shall be, Near - er, my God, to Thee,
Yet in my dreams I'd be Near - er, my God, to Thee,
An - gels to beck - on me Near - er, my God, to Thee,
So by my woes to be Near - er, my God, to Thee,

Near - er, my God, to Thee, Near - er to Thee.

Alice Cary.

Moderato.

Arr. from Franz Abt.

1. There is hov - er - ing a - bout me A power so sweet, so

1. There is hov - er - ing a - bout me A power so sweet, so

sweet, I know, de - spite my sor - row, That we shall

sweet, I know, de - spite my sor - row, That we shall

pp

sure - ly meet, . . . That we shall sure - ly meet.

sure - ly meet, That we shall sure - ly meet.

THERE IS HOVERING ABOUT ME.

2. I know, and thus the dark-ness Be - tween us is de -
4. You send me in - ti - ma - tions In morn-ing's gen - tle

2. I know, and thus the dark - ness . . . Between us is de -
4. You send me in - ti - ma - tions . . In morn- ing's gen - tle

fied, That death is but a shad - ow, That
beams, And at night you come and meet me, And at

fied, That death, That death is- but a
beams, And at night, at night you come and

That death is but a shad ow, That
And at night you come and meet me, And at

death is but a shad - ow, With sun - shine ei - ther
night you come and meet me In the gold - en gate of

shad - ow, is but a shad - ow, With sun - shine ei - ther
meet me, you come and meet me In the gold - en gate of

death is but a shad - ow, With sun - shine ei - ther
night you come and meet me In the gold - en gate of

side, With sun - shine ei - ther side. 3. The world is ver - y
dreams, In the gold - en gate of dreams.

side, With sun - shine ei - ther side. 3. The world is ver - y
dreams, In the gold - en gate of dreams.

wea - ry, But I shall ev - er know That still there is a

wea - ry, But I shall ev - er know That still there is a

borderland Where spirits come and go, Where spir - its come and go;

borderland Where spirits come and go, Where spir - its come and go;

John Burroughs.   E. W. Foster.

Moderato sostenuto.

Se -
rene I fold   my hands and wait,   Nor care for wind, or   tide, or sea.   I
rave no more 'gainst time or   fate,   For lo! my own   shall come to   me.   I

8ᵛᵃ mf a tempo.

stay my haste, I make de - lays, For what a - vails this ea - ger pace? I
stars come nightly to the sky; The ti - dal wave un - to the sea; Nor

mf a tempo.

con passione.

stand, a - mid th'e - ter - nal ways, And what is mine shall know my face, I
time, nor space, nor deep, nor high, Can keep my own a - way from me, Nor

cres.

mf   cres.   poco a poco.   rall.   sf   sf   FINE.

stand a - mid th'e - ter-nal ways, And what is mine shall know my face.
time, nor space, nor deep, nor high, Can keep my own a - way from me.

mf   cres.   poco a poco.   rall.   sf   FINE.

MY OWN SHALL COME TO ME.

A - sleep, a - wake, by night or day The friends I seek are seek - ing

me; No wind can drive my bark a - way, Nor change the tide of des - ti -

ny. What mat - ter if I stand a - lone? I wait with joy the com - ing

years; My heart shall reap where it has sown, And gath - er up its fruits of tears: My heart shall reap where it has sown,   And gath-er up its fruits of tears.

The wa - ters know   their own and   draw The brook that

springs from yon - der   height; So flows the   good with   e - qual

law Un - to the   soul, the   soul of   pure de - light.   The

ANGEL OF PEACE.

Oliver Wendell Holmes.

Matthias Keller.

1. An - gel of Peace, thou hast wandered too long! Spread thy white wings to the
2. Brothers we meet, on this al - tar of thine Ming - ling the gifts we have
3. An - gels of Beth - le - hem, an-swer the strain! Hark! a new birthsong is

1. An - gel of Peace, thou hast wandered too long! Spread thy white wings to the
2. Brothers we meet, on this al - tar of thine Ming - ling the gifts we have
3. An - gels of Beth - le - hem, an-swer the strain! Hark! a new birthsong is

Maestoso. ♩ = 76.

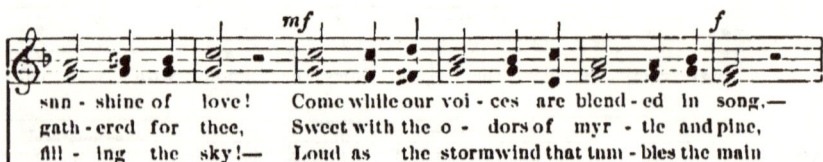

sun - shine of love! Come while our voi - ces are blend - ed in song,—
gath - ered for thee, Sweet with the o - dors of myr - tle and pine,
fill - ing the sky!— Loud as the stormwind that tum - bles the main

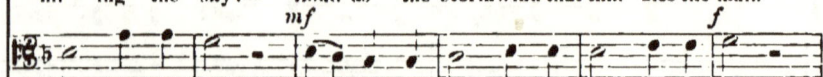

sun - shine of love! Come while our voi - ces are blend - ed in song,—
gath - ered for thee, Sweet with the o - dors of myr - tle and pine,
fill - ing the sky!— Loud as the stormwind that tum - bles the main

Fly to our ark like the storm-beat-en dove! Fly to our ark on the
Breeze of the prai - rie and breath of the sea,— Meadow and mountain and
Bid the full breath of the or - gan re-ply,— Let the loud tem-pest of

Fly to our ark like the storm- beaten dove! Fly to our ark on the
Breeze of the prai - rie and breath of the sea,— Meadow and mountain and
Bid the full breath of the or - gan re-ply,— Let the loud tem-pest of

wings of the dove,— Speed o'er the far-sounding bil-lows of song,
for - est and sea! Sweet is the fragrance of myr-tle and pine,
voi - ces re - ply,— Roll its long surge like the earthshaking main!

wings of the dove,— Speed o'er the far-sounding bil-lows of song,
for - est and sea! Sweet is the fragrance of myr-tle and pine,
voi - ces re - ply,— Roll its long surge like the earthshaking main!

Crowned with thine ol - ive - leaf gar - land of love,— An - gel of
Sweet - er the in - cense we of - fer to thee, Broth-ers once
Swell the vast song till it mounts to the sky!— An - gels of

Crowned with thine ol - ive - leaf gar - land of love,— An - gel of
Sweet - er the in - cense we of - fer to thee, Broth-ers once
Swell the vast song till it mounts to the sky!— An - gels of

Peace, thou hast wait - ed too long!
more round this al - tar of thine!
Beth - le - hem, ech - o the strain!

Peace, thou hast wait - ed too long!
more round this al - tar of thine!
Beth - le - hem, ech - o the strain!

MY BIRTHDAY.

John Greenleaf Whittier.   Johann Friedrich Reichardt.

1. Be - neath   the   moon - light   and   the   snow,   Lies
2. I   grieve   not   with   the   moan - ing   wind   As
3. Not   mind - less   of   the   grow - ing   years   Of
4. The   years   no   charm   from   Na - ture   take;   As
5. Rest   for   the   wea - ry   hands   is   good,   And
6. Let   winds   that   blow   from   heaven   re - fresh,   Dear

dead   my   lat - est   year;   The   win - ter   winds   are
if   a   loss   be - fell;   Be - fore   me,   e - ven
care   and   loss   and   pain,   My   eyes   are   wet   with
sweet   her   voi - ces   call,   As   beau - ti - ful   her
love   for   hearts   that   pine,   But   let   the   man - ly
Lord,   the   lan - guid   air;   And   let   the   weak - ness

wail - ing   low   Its   dir - ges   in   my   ear.
as   be - hind,   God   is,   and   all   is   well!
thank - ful   tears   For   bless - ings   which re - main.
morn - ings   break,   As   fair   her   even - ings   fall.
hab - i - tude   Of   up - right   souls   be   mine.
of   the   flesh   Thy   strength of   spir - it   share.

THE POET AND THE CHILDREN.

John Greenleaf Whittier.   Ferdinand Gumbert.

1. With a glo - ry of win - ter sun - shine
2. It came from his own fair cit - y From the
3. The lays of his life's glad morn - ing, The
4. With a sense of awe he list - ened To the

O - ver his locks of gray, In the old his - tor - ic
prai - rie's bound - less plain, From the Gold - en Gate of
psalms of his eve - ning time, Whose ech - oes shall float for -
voi - ces sweet and young; The last of earth and the

. man - sion, He sat, on his last birth-day; (BASS) With his
sun - set, And the ce - darn woods of Maine. (BASS) And his
ev - er On the winds of ev - 'ry clime. (BASS) All their
first of heav'n Seem'd In the songs they sung. (BASS) And

(Sop.) 1. With his books and his pleas - ant pic - tures, And his
(Sop.) 2. And his heart grew warm with - in him, And his
(Sop.) 3. All their beau - ti - ful con - so - la - tions, Sent
(Sop.) 4. And wait - ing a lit - tle long - er For the

books and his pleas - ant pic - tures, And his house - hold and his
heart grew warm with - in him, And his moist - 'ning eyes grew
beau - ti - ful con - so - la - tions, Sent forth like birds of
wait - ing a lit - tle long-er For the wonder-ful change to

house - hold and his kin,
moist - 'ning eyes grew dim,
forth like birds of cheer,
won-der-ful change to come,

CHORUS.

kin, and his kin, ' While a sound as of myr - i - ads
dim, eyes grew dim, For he knew that his coun - try's
cheer, birds of cheer, Came flock - ing back to his
come, change to come, He heard the sum - mon-ing

sing - ing From far and near stole in, While a
chil - dren Were sing - ing the songs of him: For he
win - dows, And sang in the po - et's ear, Came
An - gel, Who calls God's chil - dren home! He

sound as of myr - i - ads sing-ing From far and near stole in.
knew that his coun - try's chil - dren Were sing-ing the songs of him.
flock - ing back to his win - dows, And sang in the po - et's ear.
heard the sum - moning An - gel, Who calls God's chil - dren home.

A PSALM OF LIFE.

Henry Wadsworth Longfellow.   Henry Smart.

1. Tell me not in mournful num-bers Life is but an emp-ty dream! For the soul is dead that slum-bers, And things are not what they seem, And things are not what they seem. Life is re-al! Life is ear-nest! And the grave is not its goal; Dust thou art, to dust re-turn-est, Was not spo-ken of the soul, Was not spo-ken of the soul.

2. In the world's broad field of bat-tle, In the biv-ou-ac of Life, Be not like dumb, driven cat-tle, Be a he-ro in the strife! Be a he-ro in the strife! Trust no fu-ture how-e'er pleas-ant; Let the dead past bury its dead! Act— act in the liv-ing pres-ent! Heart within and God o'er-head, Heart within, and God o'erhead!

3. Lives of great men all re-mind us We can make our lives sub-lime, And, de-part-ing, leave be-hind us Footprints on the sands of time;— Footprints on the sands of time;— Foot-prints, that perhaps an-oth-er, Sail-ing o'er life's sol-emn main, A for-lorn and shipwreck'd broth-er, See-ing, shall take heart a-gain, See-ing, shall take heart a-gain.

Fanny Crosby.   George Frederick Root.

Moderato.

1. There's mu - sic in the air . . When the in - fant morn is
2. There's mu - sic in the air . . When the noon-tide's sul - try
3. There's mu - sic in the air . . When the twi- light's gen - tle

nigh, And faint its blush Is seen On the bright and laughing sky.
beam Re - flects a gold - en light On the dis - tant moun-tain stream.
sigh Is lost on eve - ning's breast As its pen - sive beau - ties die.

Many a harp's ec - stat - ic sound, With its thrill of
When, be - neath some grate - ful shade, Sor - row's ach - ing
Then, O then the loved ones gone Wake the pure, ce -

* A good effect is produced by playing this part an octave higher.

joy pro - found, While we list en - chant-ed there To the
head is laid, Sweet-ly to the spir - it there Comes the
les - tial song; An - gel voi - ces greet us there In the

mu - sic in the air.
mu - sic in the air.
mu - sic in the air.

2d time pp.

2d time pp.

2d time pp.

INDEX.

www.ingramcontent.com/pod-product-compliance
Lightning Source LLC
Chambersburg PA
CBHW030841270326
41928CB00007B/1153